D1020512

Early praise for *Small Message, Big Impact*®

"Terri's book brings a fresh, relevant, and much needed update to the topic of Elevator Speeches . . . and her real world, practical approach gives readers the understanding, and the tools to use this material immediately to generate real results! Well Done!"

—Daniel Burrus, CEO, Author, Technotrends

"More than just a "feel good" or motivational book, *Small Message, Big Impact*® offers a unique blend of academic thought, logical organization and real world experience. Terri has done a great job of keeping readers engaged while providing them with information and skills they can use immediately."

—Jerry Cox, President Total Training Network/Peak Performers

"Whether you're an entrepreneur pitching an idea to a venture capitalist, an account executive focused on closing the sale of the year or an individual seeking the next chapter of your career, Terri Sjodin's Small Message Big Impact guides you every step of the way to build and deliver the perfect elevator speech . . . a tool that can be the difference between a deal maker and a deal breaker."

—Charlie Frankel, Senior Vice President of Sales and Marketing
Larry Blumberg and Associates, Inc.

"Presentation isn't everything, but it is the main thing. Whether in business or in life, influence matters. Terri's newest book blows up the myths of selling and presenting and gives a fresh and highly effective solution for winning people to your cause and adding value to their life."

—Todd Duncan, Chief Performance Officer
Todd Duncan is the *New York Times* bestselling author of
High Trust Selling: Make More Money in Less Time with Less Stress
and *Time Traps: Proven Strategies for Swamped Salespeople.*

"Being able to tell your story is critical . . . the ability to share your message quickly and succinctly is essential. In *Small Message, Big Impact*, Terri Sjodin expertly teaches you how to do both."

—Erin K. Casey, contributing editor at *SUCCESS* magazine
and author of *Zany Zia's Hats to Where*

"Customers are inundated with messages of buy, buy, buy! - From me, me, me! Are you struggling with a message as to why they should buy from you? Terri Sjodin's book *Small Message, Big Impact*° provides the reader with an easy, step-by-step approach to create a memorable and compelling story that will get you more time in front of your customer."

—Scott Hinkle, Director – North America Training,
CIBA VISION° Corporation

"*Small Message, Big Impact*° by Terri Sjodin provides a straightforward, practical how-to manual on effectively delivering and communicating your critical message in your own voice. Terri not only lays out a clear methodology for delivering a brief presentation that will generate real results, but also provides genuine, heartfelt advice on how to be a better communicator in life. I would recommend this book to all who want to improve their speaking ability, but also want to make a real difference and impact in the world."

—William Hicks, Franklin Consulting Group

"Terri weaves critical techniques with great examples throughout this book. A must read for anyone who wants to hone their presentation skills and make a real connection with their audience. Bravo!"

—Chris Kervandjian, Vice President International Services &
Operations, Century 21 Real Estate, LLC

"In the few minutes we have on the House Floor before a vote, successfully utilizing what Terri has written about can mean the difference between a piece of legislation passing or failing. The ability to succinctly and convincingly give an elevator-speech is essential to the success of any political or business figure. Building on the lessons from her first book, Terri has put forward a must-read for anyone who is in the business of selling something."

—Darrell Issa, U.S. Congressman (CA-49) Ranking Member on the
Oversight and Government Reform Committee

"Terri Sjodin hits a "home run" with *Small Message, Big Impact*®. From planning to practice and from presentation to successful conclusion, she lays out a clearly defined path to becoming a better communicator. Terri provides the necessary practical steps and techniques, and I recommend this book to anyone interested in bettering their own communications skills. Everyone benefits from improved communication."

—Kevin Maguire, Manager of Travel for Athletics, University of Texas Austin Chairman-National Business Travel Association

"Terri has the ability to teach you how to use your own authentic voice when you deliver a speech or message. She challenges you to create your own path, continue to improve and grow, enjoy the ride by being creative and scrappy, above all enjoy the ride!"

—Tom Bardenett, Executive Vice President, Interstate Hotels & Resorts

"Most of us in sales flood customers with information. Terri helps professionals build a practical persuasive case, and still speak with their own natural style and voice."

—Chris Nelson, CPT Divisional Vice President Ameriprise Financial

"Terri Sjodin's "Small Message has made a Big Impact" on our entire organization. Her approach provides a professional "persuasive build your case" approach that prospects and clients appreciate and respect. If nothing else, Chapters 2 and 5 will change your perspective on presentations and what you need to do NOW to change your approach. Trust me; it works! Our sales are up over last year even in this sluggish economy."

—Jerry Anderson, CCIM, Sperry Van Ness, Florida

"Small Message Big Impact should be a must read for every organization that is serious about improving their sales and project development areas. Finally, a "how to" book that is easy to understand in terms of steps. Brilliant!"

—Dean Rodewald, Vice President Matrix Financial Solutions

Small Message, Big Impact

Small Message, Big Impact

HOW TO PUT THE POWER OF THE ELEVATOR SPEECH EFFECT TO WORK FOR YOU

Terri L. Sjodin

GREENLEAF
BOOK GROUP PRESS

Published by Greenleaf Book Group Press
Austin, Texas
www.gbgpress.com

Distributed by Greenleaf Book Group LLC

For ordering information or special discounts for bulk purchases, please contact Greenleaf Book Group LLC at PO Box 91869, Austin, TX 78709, 512.891.6100.

Design and composition by Greenleaf Book Group LLC
Cover design by Greenleaf Book Group LLC
Scrappy Sue illustrations by Katrina Peterson
Author Photo by Brystan Studios

Sjodin, Terri L.
    Small message, big impact : how to put the power of the elevator speech effect to work for you / Terri L. Sjodin. — 1st ed.
    p. ; cm.
    Includes index.
    ISBN: 978-1-60832-130-8
    1. Business presentations.   2. Business communication.   3. Interpersonal communication. I. Title.
HF5718.22 .S56 2011
658.4/52   2010941113

Part of the Tree Neutral® program, which offsets the number of trees consumed in the production and printing of this book by taking proactive steps, such as planting trees in direct proportion to the number of trees used: www.treeneutral.com

TreeNeutral®

Printed in the United States of America on acid-free paper

11 12 13 14 15 16   10 9 8 7 6 5 4 3 2 1

First Edition

*To Nick C. Taylor, my sounding board,
my walking partner, my confidant,
and one of my best friends*

contents

acknowledgments

The cool part about the acknowledgments page is that it's the author's chance to formally thank the people who have supported the writing of her book. It's important because this work is the combined effort of people who have come together in many different ways. No one accomplishes a goal like writing a book alone.

With sincere gratitude, I would like to thank my team, family, friends, and colleagues who have helped bring this project into form.

My editor, Kari Barlow, has been indispensable in bringing this book to life. Thank you for helping me take my speeches, lectures, and seminar writing style and convert it into this manuscript.

Sealy Yates, my literary agent, has believed in me and in this project from the start. Your guidance and suggestions, even when they were painful, have been invaluable to me.

Thanks to talented cover designer Lisa Woods, who illustrated my vision beautifully.

My national coordinators/directors of client relations through the years, Mary Jo Standley, Michelle Gulledge, and Leanne Martin, have helped keep me organized and free to move forward. Your loyalty and support are a huge part of our success.

I want to thank my mentors and coaches for their guidance and support. You were generous enough to share with me your pearls of wisdom to help me navigate the hills and valleys of my journey.

My critical review team took the time to read the early drafts and provide wonderful feedback. Thanks to Susan Suffes, who helped me to craft the initial proposal for this work, and to Linda O'Doughda, who copyedited it. Each of you has helped me make this book a valuable tool for the readers.

I would also like to express my deep appreciation to the many corporations, associations, and individuals who have included my programs in their training and development agendas. Much of this material has been crafted from the real world: field-tested presentation experiences in those workshops and courses.

A very special thank-you goes out to my colleagues and friends at the National Speakers Association and Gen Next.

My parents, Jan and Pete Sjodin, my sister, Kim, and my extended family members were all part of the manuscript review team at one time or another. You and your efforts are loved and appreciated.

My dearest friends, old and new, are all such a wonderful gift. On this particular project, I want to give a "shout out" to Colette Carlson, Peter Huber, Nicole Najoan, Pattie Scoma, Amy Jones, Kristin Henriksen, Joey Walker-Bialek, Renee Raithel-Gabbard, Nick Taylor, and Brad McMillen for their time and consistent willingness to let me share the bits and pieces along the way and for their opinions and contributions.

November 15, 2010, marked Sjodin Communications' twentieth anniversary! I am blown away at how quickly the years have passed. I am honored and humbled to have been able to build this little company and make a living doing what I love to do. Thank you all for being part of my journey. I am so truly grateful for the blessings I have received.

preface

I was a member of the speech and debate team in high school and in college. Formally, it was called competitive forensics. Informally, I was a "speech geek." When I look back at those years, I realize how fortunate I was to have had such incredible speech team coaches. At Fountain Valley High School, Jim Caforio encouraged me to train and compete in speech tournaments. In my freshman and sophomore years at Orange Coast College, I was truly blessed to have had a sharp and really tough debate coach named Peg Taylor. With her amazing guidance I became a successful policy debater in the National Forensic League's (NFL) Lincoln Douglas Debate. I must confess there were times she pushed me so hard I would cry tears of frustration that I just couldn't get it, but I would not be where I am today without her incredible "No B.S." coaching and instruction on crafting a persuasive case.

In my junior year I transferred to San Diego State University where I worked with Coach Paul Gaske. Paul showed me how to find my own voice and style when presenting and helped me get to the NFL nationals in persuasive speaking in both my junior and senior year. Those years of core classic training gave me a sense of comfort and a secure foundation from which to apply this skill set to the business world and to grow professionally in sales and as an entrepreneur. Now, more than twenty years later, I look back with humble gratitude for the impact those coaches had on my life. Be careful whom you call a speech geek, lest you flatter her!

MY FIRST ELEVATOR SPEECH

My first elevator speech experience was by complete accident. I had no idea what an elevator speech was or if the term was even around back then. If you have read my book *New Sales Speak* (John Wiley & Sons, 2006 second edition), you will be familiar with this story. This version gives you a slightly different perspective, however.

In 1987, I was a straight commission sales representative for a small company called the Achievement Group, which represented professional speakers widely known for their ability to clearly communicate new and effective sales techniques. My job was to sell training and development seminars to corporate clients who needed to train and motivate their sales teams. For two years, I traveled all across the United States and promoted our events in Memphis, Cincinnati, Hartford, Miami, Minneapolis, and many other cities. My first territory was in Orange County, California. My responsibility was to cold-call companies within my territory and set up meetings and presentation opportunities. The goal was to deliver a fifteen- to twenty-minute presentation on our seminar events and to get people registered to attend.

One of the most desirable yet difficult prospects on my target list was a large residential real estate organization named Century 21 Emery. Headed by a man named Jim Emery, it was a highly successful group with nine offices, each of which had more than fifty agents. My goal was to deliver a presentation to the sales staff in each of those offices; their management policy, however, prevented outside salespeople from giving presentations during agent staff meetings. This closed door frustrated me, but it also stimulated my competitive imagination. I kept asking myself how I could possibly go around this barrier, and I even consulted my teammates in other territories for their suggestions. But my colleagues were no help. If anything, they discouraged me.

When I asked a more experienced sales professional from the Achievement Group team what he would suggest I do, he responded: "Forget it, Terri; you will never get in there. It is a closed office. Move on to the next account."

I was stuck. I questioned the difference between a closed office and an open office. (Quite frankly, I have never entered an office that had a bright flashing neon sign proclaiming: "Open to vendors and solicitors. Come on in!") The answer was that there is no difference except for the amount of time and creativity it takes to get through the door! Bummer. I knew it was not going to be easy.

Time to get a little scrappy . . .

I followed up with phone calls and mailings, but nothing happened. I changed my strategy and began meeting with each Century 21 Emery manager separately, but every one of the nine said the same thing: If I wanted to get into the office, I would have to have permission from Jim Emery himself. So I turned my attention toward getting an appointment with him. No such luck. He had a very good secretary—that is, one who had been trained to screen calls from salespeople.

The more I got rejected, the more determined I became to get inside Emery's organization. I surmised that few, if any, sales training representatives had given presentations to these people, so if I could get inside, I knew it would be a great account. But how was I going to do it?

The movie *Wall Street* gave me the inspiration for my approach. The lead character, Bud Fox, played by Charlie Sheen, delivers a box of imported cigars to his prospect, Gordon Gekko, played by Michael Douglas, on his birthday. The gift ultimately helps Fox gain access to Gekko for a brief meeting. I thought, *Hmmm, maybe I can come up with one of those creative solutions characterized in the film.* Although I was young and naïve and clearly lacking connections, I decided to buy a long-stemmed white rose and deliver it to Jim Emery in person. At the time, I felt a white rose was appropriate because it symbolized integrity. (I also was short on funds, and my company didn't provide sales-people with expense accounts.)

The only appropriate place that I could think to approach Emery was in the parking lot outside his office. At 5:30 AM, wearing my best suit, I took up sentry duty next to his parking space, which was clearly marked with his name on it. I had been waiting about an hour and a half when a car finally pulled up. The driver was obviously the man I wanted.

"Excuse me, are you Jim Emery?" I asked timidly.

"Yes, I'm Jim," he replied. "Who wants to know?"

"Just some young gal who needs about ten minutes of your time," I said. (Um, not the best response, but this is what happened.)

"What is she selling?" Emery asked, cutting to the chase.

"I don't suppose she is selling anything," I said, deferring to the obvious. "I think she just needs to deliver this flower."

The laughter that crossed his lips was a great relief. He opened the card that I had included with my gift. It read: "Mr.

Emery, please just give me ten minutes of your time. I definitely believe I have something that will be of interest to you." (Again, looking back, this was weak. He must have seen that I was really trying, though, because luckily he gave me a shot.)

"I don't have ten minutes," Emery said. "You have two minutes as we walk from this car to that door."

I really didn't have time to think it over. Every debating technique I had learned in college sprang to readiness. Instinct kicked in and I delivered my message. In about two minutes, I came up with more reasons why he would be "at a loss" if he didn't meet with me than I had used in the prior three months with all my other clients combined.

"Okay," Emery told me. "I'll give you your ten minutes. Come back tomorrow at nine o'clock."

I kept to his schedule and delivered my presentation in ten minutes. Our meeting, however, lasted one and a half hours. What exceeded my most exaggerated hopes was his sending a little note of introduction and recommendation to each of his managers permitting me to make a presentation at their staff meetings.

This was my first experience of the "Elevator Speech Effect." That forced, accidental, spontaneous elevator speech led to the one-on-one presentation with Jim Emery, which led to the opportunity to present at all nine of his offices, which ultimately resulted in my reaching my sales goals for that cycle. Yeah!

Because it worked, I tried it again and again. Looking back now, I realize that this was the beginning of my understanding of the Elevator Speech Effect. Without having a name for it back then or having a real understanding of its cause-and-effect benefits, I learned how to use this tool repeatedly to initiate a series of appointments.

This is the story behind this book. Who knew, all these years later, that this one small message would have such a big impact on my life?

I opened Sjodin Communications, a fledgling public speaking sales training and consulting firm, in November 1990—from a spare room in my home. Today, our offices are based in Newport Beach, California.

For more than two decades, I have watched the evolution of presentations. Clearly, competition for a listener's time and attention span is fierce, and the need to craft engaging talks in a short period of time has become essential. Through the years, I began to offer specialized workshops in which I coached individuals on building and delivering effective three-minute elevator speeches.

I admit, even after all this time, I still enjoy the process, and I love watching the shift in mind-set that occurs after people learn how to craft engaging talking points. I have seen people who usually wing it learn to create persuasive messages that enable them to hit the streets with renewed enthusiasm and a clear mission, and then they execute those messages with ease and flow, and they reach their goal. "I got the job." "I landed the appointment." "I got the donations we needed." "I closed the deal." The transformation and accomplishments that have occurred for individuals as a result of employing this tool have been wonderful and humbling to witness.

My faith in the elevator speech has grown so strong in the last few years that I was compelled to write a little book to help individuals craft their own messages, to shrink their learning curve, to pass on some valuable tips, and to save their sanity and a lot of their time in the process.

Now, through this book, *Small Message, Big Impact**, you can access some of my workshop material and put the Elevator Speech Effect to work for you!

Whatever your goal, be it landing a major account, getting your dream job, becoming the top sales professional at your company, or meeting the right person to help you get to where you want to go, I hope this book can help you complete your quest and have a lot more fun on the journey.

concept

The Elevator Speech +
The Butterfly Effect =
The Elevator Speech Effect

You're in the airport waiting for a flight, burning time by checking your BlackBerry or iPhone and reading the paper. You just want to get home. Then you catch a glimpse of the CEO of a company you have wanted to meet with for weeks. He's standing against the wall, also waiting for his flight. *Your* flight! Hmmm, wouldn't it be great if you were seated next to him? Should you walk over? What would you say? You don't want to be intrusive, but gosh, it's a great opportunity to talk with him and introduce yourself. There's no secretary to screen you out. All you have to do is walk over and hand him your card.

Your pulse quickens and your mind races. *What will I say?* you ask yourself. *I'll leave him alone.* You decide he doesn't want to be bugged. Then, over the loud speaker, you hear first class passengers invited to board the plane. He is gone, and so is your shot. Bummer.

Stop. Rewind. Let's play that again with a new ending.

You're in the airport waiting for a flight, burning time by checking your BlackBerry or iPhone and reading the paper. Then you catch a glimpse of the CEO of a company you have wanted to meet with for weeks. He's standing against the wall, also waiting for his flight. Your flight! Hmmm.

This time you are calm, cool, and collected. Like Frank Sinatra, you casually stroll over and stand next to him and strike up a conversation. There is a bit of pressure, but you can calmly control the pace and your nerves. Yes, it is true you are running short on time, and you know that they will call the first class passengers to board soon, but you are careful to not be too aggressive ("Don't scare the bunny!"). At just the right moment, you gracefully transition into your setup, introduce yourself, and share your elevator speech in a relaxed and conversational manner. He is amused and intrigued.

Wouldn't it be great if you were seated next to him? You're not. But that's OK. You don't want to be intrusive, so you wait to see if he shows any interest or asks a question. When he does, you ask for an opportunity to follow up and set up an appointment for a future date that could be more convenient. He pauses and reaches for his card. You hand him yours and wrap it up, gracefully transitioning back to a casual conversation and wishing him a nice flight. Beautiful. Clean. Professional. Classy.

You follow up appropriately after you get home and back to work. He agrees to a phone conversation, and you set up an appointment. The Elevator Speech Effect is in motion and many possibilities await you. I think you will agree that this scenario has a much better ending—or should I say beginning?

INTRODUCING THE ELEVATOR SPEECH EFFECT

ELEVATOR SPEECH (N.)—AN ELEVATOR SPEECH IS A BRIEF PRESENTATION THAT INTRODUCES A PRODUCT, SERVICE, PHILOSOPHY, OR AN IDEA. THE NAME SUGGESTS THE NOTION THAT THE MESSAGE SHOULD BE DELIVERED IN THE TIME SPAN OF AN ELEVATOR RIDE, UP TO ABOUT THREE MINUTES. ITS GENERAL PURPOSE IS TO INTRIGUE AND INSPIRE A LISTENER TO WANT TO HEAR MORE OF THE PRESENTER'S COMPLETE PROPOSITION IN THE NEAR FUTURE.

—TERRI L. SJODIN

The short conversational message you shared with the dream client in the middle of that busy airport is an example of what's known as an elevator speech. (In your world, it might not be a CEO. It could be any decision maker you want to access.) I define the term as a brief presentation that introduces a product, service, philosophy or an idea. The name suggests that the message should be delivered in the time it takes to ride an elevator up or down several floors; anywhere from thirty seconds to about three minutes. Its general purpose is to intrigue and inspire a listener to want to hear more of the presenter's complete proposition in the near future.

So what is the Elevator Speech Effect? My concept of the Elevator Speech Effect was actually inspired by MIT mathematician and meteorologist Edward Lorenz's notion of the "Butterfly Effect." That phenomenon, backed by the laws of physics, suggests that a small change on one side of the world could result in a massive difference on the other side. For instance, the flutter of a single butterfly's wings in one hemisphere could change the path of a tornado in the opposite hemisphere.

In an article titled "The Meaning of the Butterfly: Why Pop Culture Loves the 'Butterfly Effect' and Gets It Totally Wrong" in the June 8, 2008, edition of the Boston Globe, science journalist Peter Dizikes wrote: "In today's culture, the 'Butterfly Effect' has become a metaphor for the existence of seemingly insignificant moments that alter history and shape destinies. Typically unrecognized at first, they create threads of cause and effect that appear obvious in retrospect, changing the course of human life or rippling through the global economy . . ."

In *Small Message, Big Impact**, I apply the Butterfly Effect principle to the elevator speech and show you how to use this powerful little tool in your own life to obtain measurable results. The impact and almost magic ripple effect of a well-crafted and beautifully delivered three-minute elevator speech in today's changing and challenging market cannot be denied. On a fundamental level, we all understand how big efforts in small, subtle ways can make an enormous difference.

Although we cannot always track the direct link that occurs, we can begin asking the question, "What would have happened if I hadn't delivered that first elevator speech, the one that got the snowball rolling?"

one

The Elevator Speech: A Small Message Can Have a Big Impact

Do you remember *Pong*, one of the first video games? When it came out in the early 1970s, my sister and I thought it was incredibly exciting. A bulky box was attached to a TV, and by using controls on the box, you could play a very simple, repetitive game that never changed: back and forth, Bonk! Bonk! and, for a real challenge, you could (wow!) increase the speed.

As strange as it may seem now, that game galvanized people. You may recall that at the time computers were huge, noisy machines kept in rooms to themselves. So, taking one out of its environment and playing a game on it at home was an enormous technological leap.

That was then. Today, Wii is a gaming system so different from *Pong* it might have come from outer space. Equipped with a wireless controller, the Wii can also receive Internet messages and updates while in standby mode. With Wii you can watch videos, play sophisticated games, and even follow an exercise program.

Wii exists because somebody dared to expand the original vision of the computer and of computer games.

In my experience, the elevator speech has made a similar transformation. When you expand your vision of what it can do, the elevator speech becomes a powerful communication tool that can act as your personal bridge to the future you envision.

This is where the evolved elevator speech meets the concept of the Butterfly Effect. When one person delivers a three-minute elevator presentation to another person, and that person is interested and intrigued by the message, it can lead to a more in-depth conversation, which can lead to another appointment, which can lead to the two people working together in some capacity, which can lead to a long-term relationship or partnership, which can lead to more opportunities, and so on. Thus, the Elevator Speech Effect.

So how do we put the Elevator Speech Effect to work for you? Let's begin by exploring what today's elevator speech looks like.

TIME FOR A NEW LOOK AT THE ELEVATOR SPEECH

What is your current perception of an elevator speech? Is it the old-school notion of a quick-hit, informative commercial, or is it today's more precise, persuasive, intriguing tool with far more capability?

I have heard the term referred to by many people as one or more of these concepts:

❖ An icebreaker used to open a conversation and to tell someone what you do for a living

❖ A sound bite derived from an interview or a speech that has already taken place

❖ A speed date that functions as a way to introduce people for a brief period of time for one obvious purpose

❖ A fifteen-second escalator pitch that is an even shorter version that shares "your value proposition" with people

❖ A little something that you can do off the top of your head

❖ A one-size-fits-all tool for every occasion

❖ A short version of the whole enchilada of what you want to say

❖ A proposition designed to close a deal in thirty seconds

These concepts, in whole or in part, represent earlier phases or generations of the elevator speech, much as *Pong* was a first-generation video game. But just as *Pong* has evolved into today's more sophisticated Wii games, the elevator speech has morphed into a more versatile version. It has undergone a dramatic transformation into a sleek tool of precision. The elevator speech changed because the world, growing larger and more connected, demanded it. In the sections ahead, we will discuss how the new generations of elevator speeches are being used to capitalize on opportunities in academics, traditional sales, performing arts, finance, and many other areas.

THE EVOLUTION OF THE ELEVATOR SPEECH

Why is exploring this evolution so important? Because life is busier, more crowded, and more competitive. We must earn the opportunity to be heard in today's market. Think for a moment about all the people who want your attention. From the time you wake up in the morning until you turn off the light at night, you are inundated with phone calls, e-mails, and verbal requests. You deal with memos, reports, direct-mail pieces, and other hard copy—all in addition to the meetings you must attend!

It's challenging enough to give your full attention to anyone for any sustained amount of time. How can you hope to grab someone else's attention when you want to showcase what your company, or you, can do for someone else? People have little time to spare. Rivalry is rampant, whether from companies offering the same products or services as yours or charities seeking your contributions. Sure you have something to say or a product to sell, but that doesn't mean people are lining up to hear about it. In a competitive market, you are not entitled to a person's time and attention. That means you must get serious about earning the right to be heard and making those three minutes count.

Over the years, I've found that it takes approximately three minutes to establish rapport with someone and build an intriguing message. Plus, a person will usually give you that amount of time if you ask for it. Wouldn't you give someone three minutes?

What if you were able to craft a knock-it-out-of-the-park message, deliver it in three minutes or less, arouse the interest of a decision-making listener, and open up a new world of possibilities? Wouldn't you do it?

Maybe your goal is a certain job or access to a business opportunity. Perhaps you want to promote an idea, a project, or a concept. Or maybe it is your responsibility to train your team or your associates to present your message more effectively. Whatever your purpose, be it professional, academic, political, philanthropic, or personal, you can earn the opportunity to be heard. You can bridge the gap between the goals you set and generating the results you want when you apply the principles of the Elevator Speech Effect.

THE POWER AND PURPOSE OF THE ELEVATOR SPEECH

The elevator speech I know is a concise and persuasive presentation, delivered in approximately three minutes, to a decision maker, a peer, or a potential customer. The intention is to obtain a longer, more in-depth meeting during which you can deliver your even more complete sales presentation or proposition. When your elevator speech is successfully executed you begin to benefit from the Elevator Speech Effect.

The elevator ride is a metaphor for unexpected access to someone you want to sell on some idea, project, or initiative. It is not the actual length of time it takes to ride in an elevator, but rather the spirit of the clear, brief, and persuasive messaging delivered in a short period of time that I'm talking about.

Today's elevator speech has several fundamental characteristics:

❖ It can be formal or informal.

❖ The typical length is approximately two to three minutes (depending on the circumstances).

❖ It is a clear, brief message with intention.

❖ It has a sole function, which is to intrigue a listener and obtain his or her interest, therefore winning the speaker the chance to offer a longer, more detailed presentation at a later time.

❖ It has structure.

❖ It has a close.

❖ It is a tool that helps you earn the right to be heard.

❖ It can, most important of all, initiate a sequence of events resulting in dramatic and amazing opportunities, both large and small, far into the future.

THE ELEVATOR SPEECH
GOES MAINSTREAM

Fund-raisers, sales associates, housewives, entrepreneurs, artists, and academics all make use of the elevator speech for a good reason: It works! A compelling and carefully crafted elevator speech has the power to bridge the gap between nice ideas in theory and concrete results. Today's mini-presentation has reached an entirely new level. Its duration has increased to approximately two to three minutes. It is persuasive, not just informative, and at times in this competitive world, it is used to weed out the average performers from the exceptional performers in a matter of minutes.

Here are some examples of how the more formal elevator speech has evolved from a simple thirty-second commercial to a true competitive benchmark.

Entrepreneurial Example

The "Make Mine a Million $ Business" program, founded in 2006 by Count Me In with OPEN American Express, helps entrepreneurial women whose goal is to build and grow their businesses to a million dollars or more. Participants in the organization's M3 Race compete for award packages that include everything from mentoring and access to financing to business coaching and cash prizes. Finalists are required to deliver a three-minute presentation about their businesses, their qualifications, and what the program could do for them. The elements of the pitch include the market for the presenter's project, growth strategies, and an ability to execute on her vision of the future. In this competition, the women must stand in front of a panel of judges as well as a live audience. The judges, along with input from an audience vote, choose the winners.

Some of the winners benefited from an alliance forged between the M3 program and the television channel QVC, which provided them with even greater opportunities. The New York competition featured the chance to pitch a product to the giant network retailer during its product search program. Winners got the chance to sell their products live during a QVC program. That potential? Enormous. According to its website, QVC reaches more than 166 million homes worldwide. This is a beautiful example of the unexpected benefits of the Elevator Speech Effect in action.

Entertainment Example

For those in the entertainment world, how to effectively pitch an idea for a television show is such a coveted skill that the LATV

Festival—an annual Hollywood event sponsored by the National Association of Television Program Executives—features a "Pitch Pit." In it, independent television show producers get two minutes to pitch a show idea to "catchers," in this case, decision makers from talent agencies, networks, cable stations, and other entertainment sources with the power to green-light a project. Pitches include everything from animal shows, green lifestyle shows, and talk and reality formats, to women-oriented broadcasting. Successful pitchers are the ones who understand the marketplace they're facing and how to leverage their message across a variety of platforms: traditional TV, mobile communications, and the Internet.

For some, the ability to succeed in front of this audience has moved far beyond being heard at the actual NATPE competition and onto a national stage. Again, behold the Elevator Speech Effect. A few years ago, several pitches were videotaped and Jay Leno ran them on *The Tonight Show*. It was fascinating to see which pitches worked while others fell flat. The audience didn't just view the speeches; they voted on them as well. Their applause signaled whether a proposed television show should be produced.

Academic Example

To give you an idea of just how compelling the idea of a successful elevator speech is in academia, consider this: The Babcock Graduate School of Management at Wake Forest University sponsors an annual elevator pitch competition, and this one literally takes place in an elevator! MBA students from schools across the United States—institutions like Duke University, Carnegie Mellon, and Harvard—compete for more than $105,000 in total awards, one of the country's top purses. But the rewards are much better than the prize money.

The competition, which began in 2000, invites participants, without handouts or props, to deliver a two-minute pitch to judges. The whole purpose is to ignite enough attention to a business idea during a twenty-eight-floor ride and become a finalist. Those who make the cut then offer a twenty-minute presentation of their business plan to venture capitalists.

Corporate Example

American Home Shield (AHS) is a corporate entity that has also embraced the elevator speech. A home warranty insurance company based in Memphis, Tennessee, with a sales staff of more than two hundred professionals, AHS sells home warranty protection policies to new homebuyers through real estate agent referrals.

One of the goals of these professionals is to speak to Realtors at a residential real estate company's weekly sales meeting. If an AHS sales associate gets this opportunity, she delivers a speech, which explains to the agents why AHS is *the* home warranty company the agents should recommend to their clients. The goal of the speech is to close for future appointments. At that time, the sales associate can set up one-on-one meetings for twenty to thirty minutes with each agent. In those personal meetings, the representative not only learns more about the agent's needs but also details how AHS can be of service in addressing those needs.

The opportunity to get those few minutes to speak has become such an important part of the AHS sales process that in 2009 the company hosted its own company-wide three-minute elevator speech competition. In this competition, each of the fifteen regions selected one regional champion and submitted the best presenter's videotape to a panel of judges. It was like merging *American Idol* with corporate America. From there, the judges narrowed down the finalists to a group of the top five presenters. Then the videotapes of the five finalists were shown at the national sales meeting general session. The entire sales team and the judges selected one winner as the AHS National Three-Minute Elevator Speech Champion.

In addition to the recognition, the winner received an all-expense paid trip for two to St. Thomas, Virgin Islands. The competition created an environment of fun, creativity, and innovation, and participants learned with and from each other.

Clearly, the elevator speech can be effective in starting a new business, launching a television show, swaying venture capitalists, and securing company-wide sales. In addition to showing how the Elevator Speech Effect can bring wonderful surprises and opportunities, these four examples are just a glimpse of how the elevator speech also has moved far beyond the one-person-at-a-time scenario.

THE ELEVATOR SPEECH AND YOU

I want you to imagine yourself in each of the previous scenarios. Now imagine all of the other places in which you can employ an elevator speech. Do you have a fund-raising opportunity for your church, synagogue, or faith-based organization? Do you have an entrepreneurial business idea? Do you have a desire to land your dream job? Sure you do. Sometimes acting on those ideas at first seems daunting, and you don't even know where to start. The good news is that somehow it all becomes more manageable when you realize that your first step is simply to craft a three-minute message to get things rolling. And now you are beginning to understand the process of developing the tools to start making any of those things happen.

With the power to impact one person or inspire more than one person at a time and to pave the way toward future appointments, the three-minute elevator speech can be a terrific use of your time.

Imagine the benefits of speaking to twenty or thirty prospects at once versus trying to cold-call them individually, one at a time, over the phone. That's a lot more ears for a short presentation.

The three-minute elevator speech is new and improved and has the power to open doors that often remain shut. I'll put it this way: If you haven't morphed your concept of what an elevator speech really is, you're still playing *Pong*.

NEXT

The first step to a terrific presentation begins with your intentions. We will explore the significance of crafting a three-minute elevator speech designed to meet your specific intentions.

REVIEW
THE ELEVATOR SPEECH:
A SMALL MESSAGE CAN HAVE A BIG IMPACT

❖ Just as *Pong* has evolved into today's more sophisticated Wii games, the three-minute elevator speech has morphed into a more powerful tool of precision. The elevator speech changed because the world, growing ever larger and more connected, demanded it.

❖ In competitive markets, none of us is entitled to anyone's time and attention. That means you must get serious about earning the right to be heard and making your three minutes count.

❖ Today's three-minute elevator speech can be formal or informal, with a clear, brief message with intention. Its sole function is to intrigue a listener and obtain his or her interest, therefore winning the speaker the chance to offer a longer, more detailed presentation at a later time.

❖ There is no substitute for clean and concise, up close and personal communication. To be noticed, to get that chance you want, you *must* give the listener a fresh message.

❖ The perfect three-minute elevator speech doesn't happen overnight. It takes time, trial and error, creativity, and practice.

two

Define Your Intention

This is a good time to pause and ask, "What do I want to happen as a result of my elevator speech?"

To reach any goal or realize any dream, you must first define your intention. What do we mean by intention? I have researched this concept, and my favorite explanation comes from Dr. Wayne Dyer in his book *The Power of Intention* (Hay House, 2004).

Dyer puts forth what he called "a fairly common definition of intention as a strong purpose or aim, accompanied by a determination to produce a desired result." The *American Heritage Dictionary* defines intention as "a course of action that one intends to follow; an aim that guides action; an objective."

Taking these two broad definitions, let's agree that intention is the end toward which you are working. Think about the young man who arrives at his girlfriend's house to pick her up for their date. He's waiting nervously in the living room when her stone-faced father zings him with, "Son, what are your intentions toward my daughter?" The young man freezes. He has no idea what to say because all he has planned is dinner and a movie. Panic swells. Palms get sweaty. There's mumbling and stuttering. It's not pretty.

We've all been there; caught completely off guard because we had not defined our intention, and neither did we know how to articulate it. Setting an objective is essential to any course of action, any hope of being successful. Establishing a clear intention is hard work and requires careful deliberation and, ultimately, a specific set of steps to execute.

THE SIGNIFICANCE OF INTENTION

It's beneficial to keep your intention in mind at all times, not solely for when you have a presentation on the horizon. When you strike up a conversation with someone you don't know, that person doesn't have to be a designated target. Simply keep your message out there, sharing it with people who know other people. Your message is like your song, and you have to let it be heard. Believe in it, share it, and eventually, it becomes a natural part of your communication. As writer and lecturer Joseph Campbell says, "Follow your bliss and the universe will open doors where there were only walls."

YOU DON'T HAVE TO SCORE ON EVERY PLAY, JUST ADVANCE THE BALL

Now it's time to take the next step. You're focused on your intention, but life is unpredictable, and sometimes you have to be able to read a situation and adjust your course of action. I recently shared this idea with one of my dearest friends, Brad McMillen, who is a former state championship quarterback turned Internet sales executive. He offered this analogy:

> When you mentioned your concept of the three-minute elevator speech and intention, the word "intention" reminded me of when I was playing football. Our intention was to score, eventually. As quarterback, I would go to the line, ready to throw a pass. I had a system of reads, depending on the defense. The first option was to throw long. If that was covered, as I dropped back to throw, I looked at my secondary option. If he was covered, I threw to my third option. If he was covered, I just threw the ball away or ran for my life. In the end, I kept the same overall intention—score points with my team. This progression is called checking down, and it's what quarterbacks do. They check down but always with the ultimate goal of getting to the end zone. The point is you don't have to score on every play, just advance the ball. Similarly, the point of the three-minute elevator speech is not to close the deal. Its goal is to advance you to the next point in your sales process.

REALISTIC EXPECTATIONS AND OUTCOMES

What is a realistic expectation for the outcome of our elevator speech? That depends.

I think it is a little unrealistic to believe that some people will hear a general three-minute elevator speech and promptly fall all over themselves to sign the deal, buy your product, or offer you a job. It is typically best employed as a tool to advance the ball. On the other hand, there are some special complex scenarios where it might generate results more quickly than you imagined. For example, you might have seen Todd Benson's *New York Times* article "Trump Takes a Meeting, Now Backs a Resort in Brazil" on May 19, 2004, in which he tells the story of a young Brazilian entrepreneur named Ricardo Bellino who was given three minutes with Trump and, ultimately, closed a deal.

If you are like me, when you read that headline, you thought, "Wow! What did he say to Trump?" I wish we knew, but we don't, and the odds are we never will.

Sounds like a heck of an elevator speech, right? It really wasn't a miracle. It's simply an interesting example of a more complex, prepared elevator speech opportunity. Without too much trouble, you can research the story yourself and find that it is actually another lovely example of how a small message can have a big impact.

This scenario came with preset circumstances, and there was a lot more to completing the deal than just three minutes, but Bellino's three-minute elevator speech did in fact advance the ball and gained him the opportunity to move the transaction forward.

Here's how the story unfolded. Bellino was gracefully introduced to Trump by a mutual friend, John Casablancas, who wrote a letter to Trump on Bellino's behalf. This introduction, which got Bellino in the door, gave him the three valuable minutes with Trump. In his book *You Have 3 Minutes! Learn the Secret of the Pitch from Trump's Original Apprentice* (New York: McGraw-Hill, 2006), Bellino records Trump's confirmation that Bellino sold him in three minutes on the concept to build Villa Trump. However, at the end of those three minutes, Bellino went into another room and met with an executive vice president, a senior counsel for the Trump organization, and other Trump advisers.

Bellino writes: "The details were discussed to exhaustion. But the fact remains that those three minutes played a crucial role in securing the deal. If I had not been able to sell the concept of my idea in that brief period of time, Trump would have summarily dismissed me and would never have asked me to discuss the details with his assistants."

This was clearly a more complex elevator speech scenario, but Bellino had a very clear intention, and I hope that you are beginning to see the range and scope of possibilities of an elevator speech, and the magic of the Elevator Speech Effect at many levels.

So, can a listener make a decision in three minutes? Sometimes yes. Sometimes no. Sometimes you have the luxury of a planned presentation. Sometimes you're handed unexpected opportunities. If you're on your game, with an established intention and crafted message, those opportunities will not be wasted.

UNDERSTANDING DIFFERENT TYPES OF PRESENTATIONS

Within the scope of presentations, there are basically three main categories:

1. An **informative presentation** is meant to be objective. Its intention is to be unbiased and to promote learning, and it functions as cooperative rather than competitive. For example, it's a teacher's job and intention to be informative. ("Stay with me. Don't get bored, because there's an aha! moment coming up.") In an informative presentation, there is no action for the audience to take. The presenter's intention merely is to educate. For example, if you've been tapped to present the findings of a research

paper at a university banquet, your purpose is to inform the audience about the project, the key discoveries, and the results.

2. A **ceremonial presentation** appeals to the values that are cherished by a group, and its intention is to provide a sense of communion with those members of the audience. For example, it could be the toast made at a wedding by the best man or the lifetime achievement award acceptance speech at the Golden Globes. It is appropriate at a social gathering, a celebration, or a memorial.

3. A **persuasive presentation**, by design, has a very specific intention. You want the listener to take some kind of action upon hearing what you have to say. It is typically a transactional process between the presenter and the listener and should provide choice without duress. For example, if you, as a sales professional for a cosmetics company, are speaking to a group of prospects, you should introduce who you are, explain why your product line is unique in comparison to your competitor's, and state how they can buy the products directly from you today.

After reviewing the three types of presentations, I hope you can see that our elevator speech has a defined intention and falls under the persuasive category. You are working to a specific end. You are trying to get the listener to take action and book the next appointment time.

At this point, however, I often see people make the mistake of being overly informative rather than persuasive. The data-dump syndrome is one of the most common pitfalls. It's easy to do. Why? A boss, a potential customer, a friend, or a neighborhood group won't typically say no when you're only disseminating information. The problem is, they don't typically say yes, either.

NOTE: Everybody sells something, whether it's a product, a service, a philosophy, or an idea. It is possible to sell and be persuasive in a very elegant, polished manner without being overly informative.

AVOIDING THE DATA DUMP

A young woman I recently worked with reluctantly confessed that she suffered from the data-dump syndrome in her sales presentations. She was afraid of being perceived as "hard sell," and therefore, she avoided being persuasive and didn't know how to pull out the best selling points. Like many of us, she felt more comfortable in the information zone. Then she realized she had been spending a great deal of time sharing and consulting with her sales prospects without completing any transactions. Her strategy was simply to provide more information than her competitor did. She was hoping that her prospect would like her more or at least feel obligated to buy from her because she had been so thorough.

After stepping back and evaluating her presentations, she realized she needed to move beyond merely relaying information; she needed to build her case. By focusing more on brevity and tailoring her strongest points to her prospects' needs, this young professional eventually became a consistent producer in her organization.

After recognizing the danger of data dumping, you are poised to tackle any topic that comes along. Your goal is to be both informative and persuasive, pairing rock-solid information with compelling arguments. Your presentation should be a blend or a combination of the two. I have seen it play out time and again. If you are too informative, nothing happens. If you are too aggressive, nothing happens. Find a balance, and you'll see results.

INTRODUCING MONROE'S MOTIVATED SEQUENCE

So how do I find a balance between being informative and being persuasive? One of the simplest and most effective methods of clearly communicating a persuasive message with the right balance of information can be found in the work of Alan H. Monroe, who was a professor at Purdue University in the 1930s. I personally really like this formula because it's based on a clean, logical progression, not some crazy, manipulative closing tactics. In the 10th edition of the much-used textbook *Principles and Types of Speech Communication*, coauthored by Douglas Ehninger, Bruce E. Gronbeck, Ray E. McKerrow, and Monroe himself (Glenview, IL: Scott, Foresman, 1986), we learn that Monroe united two sets of procedures: "one set based on the personalized scientific method, and the other rooted in an understanding of human motivation—to form a highly useful organizational pattern . . . It is simultaneously problem-solution oriented and motivation-centered." Since 1935, that structure has been called "Monroe's Motivated Sequence" pattern. In simple terms, this means that most people, when presented with a clear challenge, will shift into a natural problem-solving mode.

As its name suggests, Monroe's Motivated Sequence is based upon the normal sequential processes of human thinking, motivating an audience or a listener to respond affirmatively to the presenter's purpose. The textbook tells us, "The Motivated Sequence is a time tested and flexible organizational pattern, one based on a speaker's two fundamental communicative concerns: a concern for creative problem solving and a concern for the audience's motives." The sequence contains five distinct steps: attention, need, satisfaction, visualization, and action. Let's take a closer look at each step and the role it plays in shaping ideas and crafting a persuasive message:

1. **Attention Step**—First and foremost, you need to gain the attention of your listeners in a favorable way by relating to the audience and setting up your talk.

2. **Need Step**—Now that you have your listeners' interest, you must make them feel a need for change. Describe the problem and support your arguments clearly with strong materials and evidence. Monroe suggests, "The psychological center of the Motivated Sequence is the Need Step—using motivational appeals together with solid evidence to stir the minds and feelings of the listener."

3. **Satisfaction Step**—Having aroused a sense of need, you satisfy it by providing a solution to the problem and showing your listeners how your plan works.

4. **Visualization Step**—Now that you have offered your plan or solution, you want to project your audience into the future so they can picture themselves enjoying the potential benefits they will receive once your plan is adopted.

5. **Action Step**—The function of this step is to translate the desire created in the Visualization Step into overt action. Tell your audience exactly what you want them to do today and exactly how to do it. Finally, briefly explain what you will do once they have made a choice to move forward.

Monroe and his coauthors explain, "The Motivated Sequence has its own internal logic aimed at satisfying audience questions: attention precedes need; need precedes satisfaction; and so on."

This pattern is extremely helpful for those crafting persuasive elevator speeches. (It helps with other messages and longer presentations as well.) When crafting the outline, the presenter should clearly see the sense of progression that the message must take in order for a listener to feel comfortable about moving forward, based on the natural processes of human thinking. Ultimately, Monroe's Motivated Sequence pattern guides a presenter to the point of advancing to the next step in the process or setting the next appointment time.

Later on I'll show you how to weave into your three-minute elevator speech outline the ideas and case points you have developed when following this sequence. Right now, I just want you to have a clearer picture of the important difference between being persuasive and being informative in your elevator speech. You will want to ask yourself, "Does my message/talk/elevator speech serve the listener by providing a clear sense of progression so he or she can feel good about saying yes?"

Capture the Attention of a Shark

Our intention is to craft talking points in our messaging that can capture the attention of the most challenging listener.

Most fishermen will tell you that to effectively catch a prize fish, you have to know what kind of bait works best. Let's say you're looking to do business with one of the top real estate attorneys in town. He's successful, busy, sharp, and ambitious. By any standard, he's a shark. So ask yourself: "What does a shark respond to? What are they like?" Cunning, skilled, competitive, brutal, and strong. He won't do business with a little pilot fish. So if you make it your goal to try and pass the shark test when crafting your messaging, there's a high probability that your messaging can work well to capture other less intimidating fish as well!

I often use this analogy to set the stage for a role-playing exercise in one of my training workshops to really bring this concept into full view. It can be a tad uncomfortable, but it's worth the effort.

CAPTURE THE ATTENTION OF
A SHARK ROLE-PLAY

THE MISSION. Imagine I have invited you to come as my guest to an industry awards luncheon. Sitting at our table will be eight other people. As I share with you the names of the other attendees, your ears perk up when I mention one person in particular, the CEO of a company you have really wanted to meet. For weeks you have tried to connect with this executive, but she's always protected behind an amazing screener or secretary. Now you are about to be gracefully introduced to this person socially at a luncheon. It's the chance you have been hoping for!

Mission impossible? Heck, no! But how are you going to transition this serendipitous meeting into a real opportunity for the future? This is exactly the kind of situation your two- to three-minute elevator speech was made for. If you give a great presentation, you will launch the Elevator Speech Effect.

Now what? You can't just jump into a pitch. You have to ease your way in. The only thing you might be able to do is spend two to three minutes and intrigue her enough to be interested in meeting with you at a different time. Be calm, not pushy, and share your message in a conversational and informal approach. The challenge is not to wing it but instead to share some key, well-thought-out talking points. Remember, this executive is a known shark, so craft your conversational elevator speech to meet the needs of a shark.

THE ASSIGNMENT. You are now given thirty minutes to prepare a two- to three-minute elevator speech for this opportunity.

Continued

YOUR INTENTION OR GOAL. Make a follow-up appointment to speak with this individual again at later date. (Just advance the ball. Don't go for the touchdown. Let's not try to accomplish that task at this point in the game, just go for the first down.)

Walk through Monroe's Motivated Sequence and ask yourself:

❖ How will I capture the attention of a shark?

❖ Why does a shark need my product, service, idea, or me?

❖ How does my plan or solution satisfy the shark's need?

❖ How will I get the shark to visualize the benefits of my plan?

❖ What is my Action Step?

Execution

You can actually run this role-play drill on your own. At Sjodin Communications, we set up an authentic (yet informal) version of the elevator speech scenario described in this exercise during an actual lunch hour. Sixteen participants were dining at two tables of eight guests each, and all of them took their turn introducing themselves and delivering their best shark pitch. After each pitch, the other participants voted either "thumbs-up," which meant "you get the next appointment," or "shake your head no," which meant "the shark probably swam past ya!"

Remember, you can clearly measure the success of your elevator speech by asking yourself after execution: "Did I meet my intention? Did what I want to have happen occur as a result of my elevator speech?"

After executing this drill the first time, most of the participants discovered that they really needed a lot more practice. They realized it was not a good time to wing it. They found they unconsciously made pointless small talk, dumped all their data, or just recited a boring list of their company's services and features. They found themselves slipping into old habits. Once they really became aware of what they were saying, everyone realized how much better their message could be using carefully crafted talking points. If the situation occurred spontaneously (which they admitted happens in one form or another every day) they could be much more prepared.

Many admitted they have had chances like this to present to a shark, and they just let them pass right by because they were intimidated and didn't know what to say. Others confessed they would start a conversation but couldn't figure out how to get it back to their intention, so nothing happened. These are all wonderful and very real confessions, but I want you to succeed in these opportune moments. Ultimately, almost everyone finds the aha! moment once they begin using Monroe's Motivated Sequence pattern to start drafting their persuasive case concepts. We will get into crafting some specific arguments in Chapter 5, but the key point to remember here is that you can avoid the data dump and build a persuasive message. The difference between being informative and being persuasive often makes the difference between advancing the ball and getting the next appointment time—or not.

GET BUSY, GET INSPIRED

Like anyone else, you have the power to change not only your own life but also the world with your own unique voice. The key is not waiting for those opportunities to come along but seeking them out. Set that meeting you've been avoiding. Get vocal at the next weekly staff meeting, and do so in a polished and elegant fashion. Share your ideas. Act on your intentions! My hope is that you will embrace your natural ability to communicate with other people, look inward for your individual strengths, and then apply them to the goals you've set.

Think of the people you admire. Maybe it's someone like actress and comedienne Jenny McCarthy, who raised awareness of a medical condition through her energetic support of Talk About Curing Autism (TACA). Where would we be if activist Alice Paul hadn't fought tirelessly for women's suffrage? Or maybe you're interested in working on global issues like activist and U2 front man Bono, who campaigns against poverty around the world. Find your inspiration and take a chance. Define your intention, share a compelling message, and make your voice heard!

NEXT

To get started on developing a winning elevator speech, you need a basic, core outline. The outline will help you structure an effective talk that has a clear introduction, strong body points, a succinct conclusion, and a powerful close.

REVIEW
DEFINE YOUR INTENTION

❖ To reach any goal and realize any dream, you must first define your intention, an end toward which you are working.

❖ Keep your message out there. Share it with people who know other people. Let it become a natural part of your communication.

❖ You don't have to score on every play, just advance the ball.

❖ An informative presentation is meant to be objective. Its intention is to be unbiased and to promote learning, and it functions as cooperative rather than competitive.

❖ A persuasive presentation, by design, has specific intent. The speaker wants his/her audience to take some kind of action upon hearing the talk. It is typically a transactional process, providing choice without duress.

❖ Use Monroe's Motivated Sequence pattern to help you design your persuasive message concepts.

❖ Your goal is to create a presentation that is both informative and persuasive and to capture the attention of the most challenging listeners.

❖ Use your voice and share your gifts and your passion.

three

The Basic Core Outline to Get You Started

I realize this chapter is not very sexy, but it contains important, functional material that you will refer to time and time again. Consider it something of a road map for the journey you are taking into the world of elevator speeches. The goal of this chapter is to help you create a core outline for any elevator speech, an outline that will give your messaging the structure it needs.

As with building anything worthwhile, structure is essential when developing a presentation. Structure allows a speaker to establish a foundation for a talk, regardless of length, and organize his or her thoughts in a logical pattern that flows easily. Structure helps you stay on point or get back on point if you wander, and it helps you tell your story. Without it, you're flying without navigation.

Structure must be paired with sound reasoning and a sense of progression. Your listeners want to know that you're heading somewhere. Think about it. Have you ever attended presentations during which you kept asking yourself, "Where on earth is this going?" When you provide them with clear progression, your listeners won't have that experience. Put another way: make it your intention to make the listener want to ask, "What happens next?" It's important to point out that the hook in your messaging is never just one word or one line. It's the whole process of drawing the listener in.

THE GOAL IS TO INFORM AND PERSUADE

We will outline our presentation with the understanding that our simple strategy is to balance our content both to inform and to persuade. Using our analytical skills, we first provide solid information that will support our arguments or talking points in the persuasive case. We will discuss building that persuasive case in greater detail in Chapter 5. For now, we must recognize that structure is essential to developing our core outline, which generates the frame for our talking points and, ultimately, our entire elevator speech.

BE PREPARED TO PRESENT USING DIFFERENT SPEAKING FORMATS

When drafting your talk, begin by choosing one of the four speaking formats:

1. An **impromptu talk** is delivered off the top of your head, using a mental outline. No specific preparations are made; the presenter typically relies on his knowledge and experience in the moment. This format provides great freedom to interact with the audience. But it can prove difficult when presenting a persuasive case because recalling just the right word or talking point from memory, with sound reasoning and a logical flow, is often challenging.

2. An **extemporaneous talk** is one delivered about a topic that you have prepared for in advance. The presentation is not written out word for word, however. Instead, your key points are drafted in an outline, which you can keep in front of you. The main benefit of using this format is that the outline serves to keep you on track and helps you remember the order of talking points and illustrations while maintaining a more conversational style.

3. A **manuscript** is used when a presentation needs to be written out word for word, and read verbatim to the audience. This method is thorough but can often sound canned and stiff, without the personal warmth and vitality of an outlined speech, unless the presenter is well rehearsed. This kind of scripting is great as a stepping-stone to preparation, but you should not carry a script with you into the field if you can avoid it.

4. A **memorized presentation** is the written manuscript committed to memory. I personally like the memorized format because it allows the speaker to focus on the audience. If you forget a segment, however, it can throw off your entire talk. You must practice, practice, practice before you execute the memorized (manuscript) speaking format.

All of these speaking formats can work even when you are delivering an elevator speech, and the one thing they have in common is the structure. And that structure is the basic, core outline, which is the same for a long presentation as it is for the elevator speech. Think of it as playing the musical instrument the accordion. The structure of the core outline stays the same, but it will expand or contract depending on how much time you have to present.

BUILDING YOUR CORE OUTLINE

When we combine a classic pattern for our core outline with Monroe's Motivated Sequence, we establish the road map for our talk, which begins with *the introduction*. The introduction should capture the listener's attention, should explain where your talk is going during the next few minutes, and should state why you are there. It sets up mental signposts in the mind of the listener. This is where you execute the Attention Step of Monroe's Motivated Sequence.

The next building block is *the body of the presentation*, which sets forth the persuasive case, establishes credibility, and typically includes three main points, which are supported by strong arguments and illustrations. This is where you can incorporate the Need Step, the Satisfaction Step, and the Visualization Step of Monroe's Motivated Sequence.

The body of the presentation is followed by *the conclusion*, which summarizes what you have just said and could, possibly, introduce a couple of additional points you wish to discuss in detail when you are given more time. Again, your goal is to intrigue the listener, complete the Visualization Step, and then gracefully transition into the close.

The final building block of the core outline is *the close*, or your specific call to action. This is where you perform the Action Step in Monroe's Motivated Sequence. You also should take time to state your personal intent—what you want to have happen as a result of the three-minute elevator speech. Ask for an appointment time so you can offer a longer, more in-depth presentation in the near future.

Developing Different Types of Talking Points

Now that you understand the basics of how to create an outline, you might be wondering if it's prudent to have more than one elevator speech. Of course! But more important, it's prudent to have a multitude of talking points that can be interchanged and substituted when circumstances change. You want to be able to customize your talking points to suit your audience.

For example, the talking points you use to gain access to a new prospect would be different from those you would use with a new client or a previous client you are trying to win back. Similarly, talking points change dramatically according to how well you know the audience and whether your listeners know your skills and capabilities.

As you begin to consider all of the places you can employ an elevator speech, you might feel a little overwhelmed. You might begin to worry that you need to redo what you've done in the past or revamp the predrafted speech your company has already provided. Don't throw those things out. I'm trying to show you how to expand your concept of how a three-minute elevator speech can work in your life. I'm trying to teach you to create your own new path, incorporating some of the best pieces from your past presentations and experiences and combining them with new ideas.

Adjusting Your Presentation Perspective

Depending on the circumstances, it's important to launch your talking points using the most relevant perspective for the listeners. One particularly successful approach is answering these three questions:

- ❖ Why should your listener choose you?
- ❖ Why should your listener choose your company?
- ❖ Why should your listener act now?

Another successful approach is the past-present-future method. Line up your talking points this way:

- ❖ Start by discussing where your audience or listener was in the past.
- ❖ Next, establish what's happening in the present, what their company is currently achieving or not achieving.
- ❖ Finally, explain how you can improve their future, where you can take them.

It's conceivable—and helpful—that you can develop talking points suitable for elevator speeches on everything from a new product your company is marketing to a new service you've added to your company's menu of options. Maybe your philanthropic organization is hosting a charity ball or golf tournament. You could develop an elevator speech to promote attendance or to ask someone to buy a ticket. Or perhaps your academic institution is sponsoring a special lecture series for students in a particular field. You could create an elevator speech to encourage people to sign up to attend. Maybe your company has undergone changes for the better. An elevator speech could help you introduce potential clients to the benefits of working with a new team. Or, you could craft an elevator speech to a recruiter explaining why he should set you up for an interview so that you might be hired for that dream job.

Condense Your Outline for Convenience

At this point, you might be asking, "Why doesn't she just give me a script to use?" It's a good question. My answer is that I do not want you to use some cookie-cutter talk that I wrote. I want you to develop your own talk in your own voice with your own creativity so that you can craft messages on your own for a variety of different scenarios.

Once you have your simple, basic outline in hand, it's important to be able to adjust it and shape it to fit the various opportunities that come your way. You might want to consider using a version that can fit on the average index card that you could have on hand for impromptu conversations. See the Blank Elevator Speech Short Outline form that follows.

NOTE: Later on, in Chapter 10, you will be given the Drafting Your Elevator Speech Long Outline Worksheet, which will help you thoroughly craft your next elevator speech.

 You can also get free downloads of worksheets by going to www.smallmessagebigimpact.com.

BLANK ELEVATOR SPEECH SHORT OUTLINE FORM (4X6 CARD)

I. INTRODUCTION
- Grab the listener's attention ....
- Tell them where you are going ....

II. BODY
- Talking point #1 ....
- Talking point #2 ....
- Talking point #3 ....

III. CONCLUSION
- Wrap up. (Allude to a couple of strong points you wish to discuss in detail if given additional time.)

IV. CLOSE: CALL TO ACTION
- Ask for an appointment time to give them a longer, more in-depth presentation.

CREATE YOUR OWN NEW PATH

I have a little place in my backyard where I write, daydream, think, read, and plan. My friends, family, and I fondly call it "Terri's Tree House." Although it is not literally in a tree above the ground, it is beautifully nestled in between a couple of trees. I love being in this simple space. I find great peace and joy in my tree house. Sometimes I invite people to join me there, but mostly it is where I go for my private Terri time.

There is no path or walkway from the main house to Terri's Tree House, just a wide, open lawn of green grass. I like walking on the grass. Oddly, this freaks out other people. I can't tell you the number of times I have invited people to the tree house and had them comment, "You need to create a path for people to walk on out to the tree house."

I say, "Why? It's OK. You can walk on the grass, it feels good."

And they say, "But you should have a path."

And I say, "It's not that far. Create your own path. You don't have to be afraid to walk on the grass."

They will then proceed with caution and finally breathe a simple, sweet sigh of relief when they reach the wooden deck of my tree house. Then we laugh.

My six-year-old niece, Mikayla, has no struggle with the grass. She runs out into the backyard with boundless energy and rolls around on it. But we adults often look for the established path, the one that's already been created by someone else. I say it's much more fun to charge ahead with the wonder of a kid and just create your own.

This applies to your presentations as well. Reexamining the structure of your talks allows you to look at the versions you've created in the past and ask yourself if it's time to create a new path. I encourage all of you to metaphorically walk on the grass, feel it between your toes, and enjoy the simple grace of nature. May this analogy inspire you to create your own new path as you develop a basic, core outline for your next presentation.

NEXT

The one thing you need to know about crafting a great speech or presentation, regardless of its length.

REVIEW
THE BASIC CORE OUTLINE TO GET YOU STARTED

❖ Structure is essential when developing a presentation. Structure allows a speaker to establish a foundation for a talk, regardless of length, and organize his or her thoughts in a logical pattern that flows easily. Structure helps you stay on point or get back on point if you wander, and it helps you tell your story.

❖ A classic, core outline is comprised of an introduction, body (typically, three main points), a conclusion, and a close.

four

It's Not One Thing, It's Three Things

We live in a world where people love to find shortcuts. The speakers and presenters I coach—who range from politicians and academics to sales professionals and entrepreneurs—are no different. They want the shortcut to crafting a great presentation in the shortest amount of time. They want to make their cases using manageable, consumable nuggets that will get their points across quickly and effectively.

Regardless of what a person might be presenting, pitching, or promoting, I often hear the same phrase followed by the same question: "Terri, I am kinda busy, so can you just tell me really fast—what is the one thing I need to know about giving a great presentation?" My response, which always is the same, goes something like this: "Okay, here's the one thing you need to know: It's not just one thing; it's three things!"

Furthermore, the term "great" is subjective. What one person thinks is great could be merely OK to someone else. So in place of great, let's go with memorable, impactful, and effective. That said, I have found that really outstanding speakers typically meet these three benchmarks:

1. **Case**—They have built solid persuasive cases, employing clean, logical arguments and evidence to support their messages.

2. **Creativity**—Their illustrations of the talking points are really creative. They have blended thoughtful analysis and storyboarding to craft intriguing and interesting messages.

3. **Delivery**—They present their messages in their own authentic voices. There's no boring professional mode; they aren't canned Stepford people (circa 1975 the classic movie, "The Stepford Wives"). Their presentation style is genuine, and people sense the truth in their delivery.

MY GOAL IS TO HELP YOU PERFORM ALL THREE BENCHMARKS WITH COMPETENCE

Some people can structure a great *case* but have a flat, boring *delivery* and no *creativity*. They're one for three. Some people have great *creativity* and polished *delivery* but have a weak *case*. They are two for three. I think you see where I'm heading with this.

I try to help people go three for three. Truly memorable, impactful, persuasive, and effective speakers and presenters hit all three benchmarks. They create a solid, persuasive, and engaging case with thought-provoking, creative, and intriguing material and stories to bring the message to life. Finally, they speak in their own authentic voice and are, therefore, believable.

Going Three for Three

The 2008 presidential election cycle was historical on multiple levels. Clearly the performances at campaign rallies, media interviews, the national conventions, and the debates left lasting impressions of each of the candidates and their running mates in the minds of the American people. I was asked daily, "Terri, what do you think of the presidential debates and the performances of the candidates?"

For the purposes of this work, I have decided to leave out my personal opinion. (Trust me, it hurts.) Instead, I chose to take a different approach. I ask that you take a look at a few of the memorable candidates through the eyes of an unbiased evaluator and try to leave your party politics and opinions aside for a moment. It's an exercise to see if you can honestly evaluate the candidates through the lens of a nonpartisan debate judge. You might just find the results fascinating!

With these simple criteria of what makes a great speaker—case, creativity, and delivery—in mind, try recalling some of the most notable performances of Barack Obama, Hillary Clinton, John McCain, and Sarah Palin. Evaluate these speakers using each of these three benchmarks individually and then decide with an unbiased opinion: Who did the best job in the election cycle speeches and debates? Who went one for three? Who went two for three? Did anybody go three for three?

History shows us that great communicators can be from any political party, either liberal or conservative. Consider John F.

Kennedy and Ronald Reagan. Can you recall other examples of three-for-three presenters today or in the past? Try applying this standard to your own speeches and the presentations you hear to gain deeper insight into what constitutes a winning elevator speech.

NEXT

Each of these three benchmarks requires individual exploration. In the next three chapters, we will discuss in greater depth what it takes to build, creatively craft, and deliver a winning elevator speech.

REVIEW
IT'S NOT ONE THING; IT'S THREE THINGS

Great speakers typically meet three primary benchmarks:

❖ Case

❖ Creativity

❖ Delivery

five

Build a Persuasive Case

In Chapter 3, we established how to create a basic outline for your elevator speech. Now it's time to make sure that it is persuasive, not just informative. This is where you will take the time to customize the talk to meet the needs of your listener and, most important, your ultimate goal of gaining more of your listener's time at a later date.

First, let's review what it is you're building. Your case must have a compelling proposition, idea, product, service, or event. Your arguments should clearly explain, albeit briefly, why your audience needs you, why they need your company or solution, and why they need it now. We want to intrigue them and tempt them a bit so that they are inspired to want to give you that next appointment time.

As usual, a great place to start is at the beginning, so ask yourself whether your elevator speech is for a planned or spontaneous situation. These two scenarios are drastically different, and each type offers its own unique challenges. Successful salespeople and business owners don't go around presenting the same kind of talk to every single prospect. They must customize, improvise, and plan.

PLANNED ELEVATOR SPEECHES

What do I mean by a planned elevator speech? I define it as any talk used in a prearranged scenario that you are aware of ahead of time. You are able to take time to prepare, study, practice, customize, and perhaps even memorize this presentation in advance. This type of speech would be useful and appropriate at a trade show, a golf tournament sponsor area, or a networking breakfast.

For all of its noise and kitsch, a convention hall is a great place to pitch a product or service over and over. It's important to remember, however, that you don't have to bore your onlookers to tears. When in doubt, opt for a more obvious approach and just throw it out there like a big softball. Try something like this:

> *"Hi there! My name is Steve. How are you today? Would you like to hear my three-minute elevator speech on these fabulous new hurricane-proof storm shutters?"*

Right up front, you've told your prospect what you're selling and how long you need his attention. You could even hold a stopwatch as a funny-but-useful tool. Some will say, "Sure." Others will say, "No thanks." Whatever the response, Steve's mini-presentation is a lot more interesting than the average approach I see at most trade shows, which usually has some stressed-out salesperson stuffing a brochure into the hands of startled passersby.

A company-sponsored golf tournament also serves as a great place to float a planned elevator speech. You're set up behind a table decorated with your company's banners and brochures, and everyone in attendance stops by to sign up for freebies or just to get a feel for the host. Again, it never hurts to be obvious and up front with your prospect. All you have to do is say:

> *"Hello, Mr. Locke. Before you get started today, may I give you my elevator speech on our new security software package?"*

It's now clear to Mr. Locke that you have a specific item to present and you don't intend to interfere with his tee time. He might say yes or he might decline, but again, your opening is better than a resigned: "How are you? Have a good game today." You probably won't get everyone to listen, but you will definitely increase your percentages.

A third example of a perfect setting for a planned elevator speech is the local networking breakfast. If you live near an active chamber of commerce, you're likely to find one of these quite easily. During the gathering, business owners are typically given a few minutes to introduce themselves. It really doesn't get any easier than this, so stand up and say to yourself, "Great, my elevator speech was made for this moment!" Then, begin with a warm and conversational transition into your brief talk. Show some humor and your quick thinking, and because of your preparation you will make contacts for follow-up meetings. Such an approach is so much more efficient than:

"Hi, my name is Bob. I've been in business for twenty years. We have the best dry cleaners in the city. Give us a try. If you're ready for a new cleaner, come see me."

This is a simple example. Earlier, in Chapter 2, we saw an example of a more complex planned elevator speech scenario in the discussion of the three-minute speech Ricardo Bellino delivered to Donald Trump.

SPONTANEOUS ELEVATOR SPEECHES

Now let's discuss the spontaneous elevator speech, the type delivered a little more on the fly. As a result, they are usually a bit trickier to navigate. They require you to always be on your toes, to always be aware of the opportunity just around the corner or likely to come up in the next turn of conversation. Once the opening is clear, you have to act quickly and confidently. In spontaneous elevator speeches such as the examples that follow, there's little room for faltering or second-guessing. If there were ever a time to blend your wit, charm, and knowledge into one solid punch, it's here.

Take Meredith, an up-and-coming interior designer, who tagged along with friends to a swanky cocktail party one evening.

She was dressed to the nines and out to have fun; she had no intention of networking at all. But then she bumped into the owner of the hottest, not-yet-finished boutique hotel in town. Meredith had been trying to get past his secretary for weeks to book an appointment. She couldn't let this opportunity slip by. Now that they were practically sharing a drink, Meredith forged ahead and said:

> *"Mr. Hightower, I am an eco-smart and energy-efficient interior designer, and I would love to share with you my three-minute elevator speech about my vision for an innovative concept for the lobby of your new hotel."*

Meredith has laid it all out there on the table—her intention and time requirement—for Mr. Hightower to see. Depending on his answer, she can pick and choose her most dazzling arguments to present in the few minutes she has.

Or take Ben, an architect out to lunch with a client. During the meal, a colleague of the client comes by to chat. After being introduced, Ben suddenly realizes he's finally face-to-face with the president of a design and engineering firm he's always admired. He's never been able to land a meeting with the woman because busy doesn't begin to describe her. He's stunned at the chance he's been handed. Ben is on the cutting edge of 3-D visualization, and he's heard that she's on the lookout for someone with his skills. What does he do? Ben makes it clear that he has something she needs:

> "Ms. Stone, this is a serendipitous moment. I have been hoping to have the opportunity to meet you. I know you are busy, but may I have a few minutes of your time to share my ideas on three-dimensional innovation and how I might be of service to you? Then perhaps we could schedule a later appointment."

Ben has established what he wants—a connection and some time—and provided his prospect with a clear idea of how much of her time he plans to take.

One final example of spontaneous elevator speeches is a scenario that happens all the time. You've arrived at your prospect's office for a meeting. A few minutes into your presentation, he likes it so much that he stops you and ushers you into his boss's office—or perhaps even introduces you to the president of the company—to brief him as well. Yes, you've been put on the spot, and yes, you must do this in only a couple of minutes, but it's a golden opportunity.

This is where deals are often made or lost. This is where the serious and prepared are set apart from the slackers. So what's your plan? Express thanks for the visit, and with laser-focus, make your prospects understand that you have something they must know more about!

IMAGINE THE NEXT STEP

Inspired by these scenarios, keep your eyes open for opportunities, both planned and spontaneous, where you can not only pitch your three minutes but also start moving beyond the greeting. While it's crucial to be able to spot openings as they come along, it's even more important to transition gracefully into your elevator speech. Think of it like building a bridge to transition from generic conversation to the real substance of your proposal.

For example, what if Steve, upon getting the go-ahead from a trade show visitor, delivers his presentation, incorporating one or even two concrete, interesting reasons his storm shutters are necessary? He might be closer to reeling in a customer to sit through the entire presentation. What if Meredith, while chatting up Mr. Hightower, offers two really clear illustrations of how she can meet a specific need he has? She might convince him she is the designer best suited to bring his hotel lobby to life. What if Ben gives Ms. Stone an elevator speech explaining how his 3-D skills can make her the envy of other firms and speed up completion time? He will be far more likely to get an interview.

So take that extra step, build the bridge, and transition from general conversation to real substance in your next talk. It will pay off, and you'll move one step closer to launching the elevator speech effect and achieving your goals.

BALANCE YOUR CONTENT

When that meeting—or three minutes—you've worked for finally comes along, you must be able to balance your content across the time allotted.

As you find yourself working within the confines of three minutes or less, every second counts. It's important to craft an elevator speech with well-timed and carefully paced pieces. In workshops, I urge students and trainees to treat their presentation outlines like math equations, propositions that exist in complete balance. You will recall the basic structure of any presentation: introduction, body, conclusion, and close. In an elevator speech, we use that same framework, creating an introduction that grabs the listener's attention; a body made up of three main points (for example, Why you? Why your company? Why now?); a conclusion; and a close. That's a total of six components to cover in our three-minute elevator speech. And in order to balance the content, we must give about thirty seconds to each component.

6 components × 30 seconds = 180 seconds, or 3 minutes.

On a longer talk of, say, 30 minutes, divide the total number of minutes by the 6 components; $30 \div 6 = 5$ minutes per section.

By adhering to this mathematical breakdown, you will be able to exert control over the clock and fight that urge to panic.

NOTE: The amount of time per segment doesn't have to be exact. This equation just serves as a nice guideline to help you find a balance among all of the talking points in your message.

Why is this so important? We are trying to avoid making lop-sided presentations that are top-heavy. A top-heavy presentation occurs when the presenter spends too much time on the front end, realizes that his time is almost up, and rushes through the middle and end of the talk. This is an ineffective use of time and why I make the point here to emphasize the math to craft a persuasive case balanced with time and content.

HOW DO I MAKE MY PRESENTATION MORE PERSUASIVE THAN INFORMATIVE?

Whether I find myself working with seasoned speakers or wide-eyed newbies, they all want to know how to make a message more persuasive. Take the example of Donna, a sales associate whose job requires that she make cold and warm calls each and every day.

"I make the calls and I try to be fresh and energetic, but lately I'm falling short of my goals. It feels like I'm just reciting the same old thing to my prospects. How can I change it up and convince them to buy?"

My answer to Donna is simple. "It always comes down to one word—need. Ask yourself this question: 'Have I defined a clear, logical case for why they really *need* me and what I am proposing?'"

What you are selling, whether your own skills, a product, an event, a service, or an idea, must come across as something your prospects need or something they care about. Otherwise, they really are just listening to you reel off facts and features and nifty little promises. They sound nice, but not compelling.

Your proposition or case must be built in such a way that it's recognized as necessary and vital to your prospect's continued success or his or her specific interests. In short, what you're putting out there has to pass what I like to call the "So what?" test.

Passing the "So What?" Test

The easiest way to explain the "So What?" test is to put it into practice. Let's take Paul, for example. Paul is a guy who has great contacts and sells advertising for an impressive and growing online magazine. When meeting with prospects, he likes to throw out that his company is number one. They also have the largest reader base in the market and lowest ad rates. Those accolades, however, haven't turned up too many clients.

Paul's problem is that simply saying his company is at the top of the food chain doesn't make it real to clients. His claims simply do not pass the "So what?" test.

Just like Paul, we must ask ourselves if we are showing our clients how our companies are poised to meet or exceed their needs. Paul can say his online magazine is more popular than any other. So what? Many people fall into this common phraseology, but it doesn't translate into anything real for Paul's prospect. His prospect wants to know how many more hourly hits he'll receive on Paul's site than on his competitor's site. Paul can say his site has the latest security protections. So what? His prospect wants to know what web analytics tools are available and what measures are in place when servers fail and cable lines go down.

Here's another example. Let's say you're in the business of house-call dog grooming. You've developed an elevator speech, have a few loyal clients, and sell yourself as providing the best customer service in three counties. So what? If I'm the busy mother of three kids and one stressed-out cocker spaniel, all I want to know is whether you'll come to my house after business hours and possibly on weekends. Best in three counties? So what? Can you save me time and gas money by showing up on my doorstep and making my dog beautiful again? If so, then maybe we have something to talk about.

Quite simply, your case or argument or presentation has to answer the following question for your listener or your prospective client: What does this mean to me? If you can answer that age-old question you're halfway to your goal of earning more of their time.

Superlatives—best, largest, oldest, newest, most popular—are wonderful tools in ceremonial speeches. They are less helpful when you are trying to persuade an audience or when you are trying to convince listeners that they need what you are offering—unless you can prove it! Your prospects come to you with their own set of specific needs and preferences. Sometimes they don't even know there is a solution until you provide it. Make certain that you are not only selling your best features but also providing useful answers to your clients' questions.

BEGINNING TO FORMULATE YOUR CASE ARGUMENT

Now that I've shown you how to begin your persuasive case, let's get down to some specifics. It's simply not enough to say you're the best. You must identify why you're the best. Think back to the main three points in the body of our outline—Why you? Why your company? Why now?—and formulate at least ten answers for each question. Again, be specific. The more distinctive your reasons are, the closer you will be to meeting your prospect's needs.

SHHH . . . THE SECRETS— SIX GENERAL CASE ARGUMENTS THAT WORK!

At this point you may be wondering, "So, what works?" In my experience several general arguments consistently work in developing an effective case. Some of these might apply to your industry and some might not. Some will work with one group of listeners and others will not. I have listed them here to get you thinking about more specific arguments that you can customize for your industry, organization, product, service, or mission.

These six case arguments have been field-tested and are based on what we hear from people, organizations, and decision makers as to what they need and want:

Time—How are you going to save them time? Your prospects don't care if you're the oldest company in your field. They want to know how your methods and processes are going to save their organizations and their people time on a daily basis. What would time savings mean to their productivity?

Money—How are you going to save them money? They don't care if you're the largest company around. They want a break on their bottom line.

Sanity—How are you going to save them mental sanity? Your prospects don't care if you're the best in your field unless you can show them specifically how you can provide effective solutions to existing problems and eliminate a certain amount of stress.

Security—How are you going to provide them solvency and security? They don't care if you have been around two hundred years. Will you be here tomorrow? They need to know that investing in you or partnering with you is a safe decision.

Fun—How are you going to help them have fun? They don't care about your staff's experience if those people have the personalities of drones. They want to know that doing business with you will be a pleasant, fun, and enjoyable experience.

Ease of use—How are you going to make things easy? Your prospects don't care that your product is the hottest and greatest technology; if it's too complicated to use, once they make the investment, they won't see any advantage in owning it.

START BRAINSTORMING YOUR ARGUMENTS

What does your message mean to your listeners? Will you save them time? Can you save them money? Can you preserve their mental sanity? Can you offer them security? Will you make life for them more fun? Will your product or service be easy to use? Answering your listener's unspoken question, "What does this mean to me?" in particular will help you really think through your ideas and craft a great case.

It might help if you actually tackle this exercise with pen and paper. What follows are three generic lists that correspond to the three main points in the body of your speech to get you started.

NOTE: Don't be too quick to throw out an idea for an argument. Sometimes you have to talk through it to discover the nugget!

Possible "Why you?" Argument Case Point Ideas

Why do they need someone with your ....? Fill in the blank with each of the following items. Then write an explanation of what that will mean for your listener or prospect. (Example: Experience—My 10 years of experience can save you a great deal of mental sanity because I can troubleshoot challenging situations for you before they become problems.)

1. Education ....
   ....

2. Tenacity ....
   ....

3. Attention to detail ....
   ....

4. Experience ....
   ....

5. Sphere of influence ....
   ....

6. Track record ....
   ....

7. Enthusiasm ....
   ....

8. Leadership ....
   ....

Add in your own ideas here . . .

9. ....
   ....

10. ....
    ....

Review your answers. Do they pass the "So what?" test? Does each answer explain, "What this means to you is . . ."? Would you be interested if you heard this case point? Can you prove it?

Possible "Why your company?" Argument Case Point Ideas

Why do they need your company's ....?
Fill in the blank with each of the following items. Then write an
explanation of what that will mean for your listener or prospect.
(Example: Location/Local servicing—Our local servicing can
save you a great deal of time because you don't have to wait for
your orders to be fulfilled from distant locations. You can walk
right in to our store and meet with the people you need to speak
with face-to-face.)

1. Longevity in the market ....

....

2. Location/Local servicing..

....

3. Technology ....

....

4. Customer service ....

....

5. Flexibility..

....

6. Commitment to excellence ....

....

7. Commitment to the environment ....

....

8. Low rates...

....

Add in your own ideas here . . .

9. ....

....

10. ....

....

Review your answers. Do they pass the "So what?" test? Does each answer explain, "What this means to you is . . . "? Would you be interested if you heard this case point? Can you prove it?

Possible "Why now?" Argument Case Point Ideas

Why do they need you, your company, your product, your service, or your solution *right now*? Fill in the blank with each of the following items. Then write an explanation of what that will mean for your listener or prospect. (Example: Special promotional discount available right now—If you opt in to our new program in the next 30 days, you will receive a 25 percent discount on all of your purchases in the next year.)

1. Special discounts ....

....

2. Seasonal needs ....

....

3. Changing market conditions ....

....

4. Needs for a fresh start with someone new ....

....

5. Better security ....

....

Add in your own ideas here . . .

6. ....

....

7. ....

....

8. ....

....

Review your answers. Do they pass the "So what?" test? Does each answer explain, "What this means to you is . . . "? Would you be interested if you heard this case point? Can you prove it?

Select One Argument for Each Talking Point

When you're finished, remember that you're crafting an elevator speech, so you can't include all of these great case points right now. Choose one argument from each of the three general lists that applies to your specific situation. You can use the other points when you make your next long presentation.

Why you? ....

....

Why your company? ....

....

Why now? ....

....

What you are left with are your three well-crafted points for the body of your three-minute elevator speech. Well done!

Remember, your talking points will change and morph depending on your audience. For example, if you are speaking to an existing contact or client, they already know you, so you most likely wouldn't use "Why me?" or "Why my company?" or "Why now?" In this case, you might say something like this:

"Mr. Jones, here's where we were last year. Here's where we are now. Here's our case for your future."

Different scenarios will require that you answer different questions in your three-minute elevator speech. I offer these general talking points to help you brainstorm how you will create your own persuasive arguments. Remember, this is your message. You should craft a case that is customized for you and your circumstances.

NOTE: Part of your burden when communicating with people is to synthesize a large amount of information and ideas into smaller, manageable, and consumable talking points. *Merriam-Webster's Collegiate Dictionary* defines synthesis as "the composition or combination of parts or elements so as to form a whole."

For instance, when selling "Why you?" you might combine aspects of your formal sales training in college, your experience on a successful athletic team, and your industry awards and recognition to build an argument that you are a solid, professional partner your prospect can rely on in a business relationship.

Ultimately, I am asking you to delve into the many facets of your material while applying your knowledge and skills for the purpose of combining elements into a pattern not clearly there before. Use words and phrases that rearrange, substitute, design, and combine elements into a new pattern to present your fresh perspective, ideas, and proposition.

CONCLUDE, AND DON'T FORGET TO CLOSE

Building a persuasive case is never complete until you attach your conclusion and back out of the presentation with a clear and confident close. Don't make the mistake of confusing the two. Each tool has a significantly different use and value. Your conclusion typically provides a quick reference back to your attention grabber, pulls loose ends together, and brings your arguments to an end.

Your presentation is not complete, however, until you close, that is, include a specific call to action. Share with your listeners what you want them to do as a result of your time together. Make the close an easy experience for the listener. (This applies to longer talks as well.) If you're human, fear of rejection might worm its way into your mind at this junction. Push past it. It might be a long shot, but it would certainly be a longer shot if you never make the request.

At this point, your one and only goal is to seek a future appointment for a longer, more in-depth presentation. Make clear what you are willing to do to make that happen and set up another face-to-face meeting.

WHAT IF I GET A LITTLE WRITER'S BLOCK?

This particular benchmark of crafting your persuasive case is essential. It will take time. Don't worry if you get a little bit stuck on your own; it's normal to experience writer's block from time to time. When this happens, it helps to brainstorm with colleagues and friends and dig into this process with a team effort. Create a "building-our-case strategy session." It can help everyone on your team if you develop your own mini–think tank.

Imagine you're just like Lt. Daniel Kaffee, played by Tom Cruise, in the 1992 movie *A Few Good Men* when he and his fellow attorneys are up all night crafting their case for the next day in court. Faced with mounting what seems like an impossible defense, they are forced to dig in and shape and reshape their points and write and rewrite their case until they get it right.

During a pivotal moment of frustration when they are struggling to find the best argument to prove their case, one of the team members, Lt. Sam Weinberg, played by Kevin Pollak, asks Kaffee, "So how are you going to do it?"

"I have no idea," Kaffee replies, visibly bouncing ideas through his mind as he searches for the answer. "I need my bat. I think better with my bat. Where's my bat?"

"I put it in the closet," says Lt. Cdr. JoAnne Galloway, another member of the legal team, played by Demi Moore. "I put it in the closet. I was tripping on it."

"It's in the closet? Don't ever put that in the closet!" Kaffee says.

Distracted and wrestling with ideas, he turns and leaves the room to retrieve the bat from the walk-in closet, which, coincidentally, forces him to notice his clothes hanging there. This triggers a new thought in his mind and leads Kaffee to an aha! moment. The magical combination of talking through his ideas with his team, in concert with retrieving the bat, helps him think better, if you will. He (quite literally in this case) changes his perspective, and that leads to the discovery of their great argument. With the argument in hand, the team begins to uncover new evidence, which ultimately leads to their winning the case.

So, don't hesitate to talk it out and change things up. Sometimes forming a building-our-case strategy session is what it takes. When you get stuck, it helps to share your thoughts and ideas with trusted colleagues and friends and spend some time in a space of creative analysis. Find your own "Thinking Bat" methodology.

"WE DO WHAT WE HAVE TO DO . . ."

So many people say to me, "Terri, it just seems so daunting!" And you know what? They're right. It's challenging at first to sit down and craft a list of your most compelling arguments. To push through this daunting task, it helps to find inspiration.

The wonderful film *The Great Debaters* inspires me. I love this movie for a host of reasons, but primarily because I'm still a speech team geek at heart. There are lots of incredible nuggets in this movie, which was inspired by the true story of a brilliant but politically radical debate team coach who uses the power of words to transform a group of underdog African American students from Wiley College into a powerhouse debate team. Coach Melvin Tolson, played by Denzel Washington, leads his students to a stunning and historic competition in which they face off with debaters from Harvard University, and win. Tolson takes his team through the journey of understanding the power of speech and debate training. He helps his team understand the significance of building a great case, employing creativity and amazing delivery, and how the range and scope of mastering this combined skill set cannot be understated.

In one scene in the film, a young man named James Farmer has just been selected as an alternate on the debate team. He's so thrilled that he runs home to tell his highly educated and successful father, played by Forest Whitaker. A strong and stern figure, Mr. Farmer congratulates his son and then says, "Extracurricular activities such as the debate team are fine, but you must not take your eye off the ball, son, so what do we do here?"

James replies, "We do what we have to do, so we can do what we want to do."

His father asks, "And what do you have to do right now?"

"My homework," James says.

"So get to it!" Mr. Farmer replies.

Leaving the room, James says, "Yes, sir."

Okay, so his dad is tough and harsh, even unnecessarily so, but that line stuck with me. "We do what we have to do, so we can do what we want to do." The same sentiment holds true in creating a great case for your elevator speech. It takes time and thought, use of your concentration and analytical skills. It demands evidence and proof and requires the ability to shape your thoughts, concepts, and ideas into a concise message. It's hard work, but in the end, it's all worth it. You do what you have to do, so you can do what you want to do.

NEXT

You've built a great case, but you still have to infuse your talk with fresh creativity and an authentic delivery. You must blend all three to have a truly great elevator speech. We need to harness the creativity that will help your message win the hearts and minds of your listeners.

REVIEW
BUILD A PERSUASIVE CASE

❖ A planned elevator speech is used in a prearranged scenario of which you are aware ahead of time. You have time to prepare, study, practice, customize, and perhaps even memorize this presentation in advance.

❖ A spontaneous elevator speech is delivered on the fly. There's no time to prepare, and it requires you to always be aware of the opportunity just around the corner or likely to come up in the next turn of conversation.

❖ Craft an elevator speech with well-timed and carefully paced pieces. Devote about thirty seconds to each segment— introduction, body with three main points, conclusion, and close.

❖ Your case must be built in such a way that it's recognized as necessary and vital to your prospect's goals, objectives, needs, or specific interests. Your claims must pass the "So what?" test.

❖ Learn how to synthesize a great deal of data to create key, persuasive arguments in your elevator speech.

❖ When you get stuck, share your thoughts and ideas with trusted colleagues and friends and spend some time in a space of creative analysis.

six

Get Creative and Bring the Message to Life

Now that we have outlined the basic structure of your persuasive case and crafted the most compelling arguments, you are one-third of the way toward developing a winning elevator speech. You've built a solid foundation from which you can communicate logical and useful ideas and ultimately call your prospects to action. As I described in Chapter 4, "It's not one thing; it's three things," you are now one for three. You've built a great case, but you still have to infuse your talk with fresh creativity and an authentic delivery. You must blend all three to have a truly great elevator speech. So let's look at the second of those three things, the subject of creativity.

WINNING HEARTS AND MINDS

This is where I want to help you tackle the challenge of being creative and livening things up. It's time to weave into your elevator speech the unique elements that will land your message squarely in the hearts and minds of your listeners. Remember, your goal is to craft a message that is memorable, influential, and effective. Now is the time you want to pique your prospects' interests and curiosity and maybe even make them laugh.

You want to present your elevator speech in a clever, witty way that lingers in the mind of each and every prospect. When they leave your presentation, it needs to stick with them, because at the end of the day, that's one way we measure a successful elevator speech. If your prospect doesn't even remember your talk, the odds of further interaction are slim, and your chances of launching the Elevator Speech Effect are significantly reduced.

HOW DO I BECOME MORE CREATIVE?

If creativity is our goal, then how do we find it? That's a difficult question to answer, because in all sincerity, it's not that easy to be creative when you're sitting behind a desk. You can't flip a switch and say, "OK, I'm going to be creative now." It's at that moment the creativity challenge presents itself. Most people look around them to see what others are doing, but merely copying your colleagues or the competition is not being creative. This point is illustrated perfectly in the highly entertaining HBO television series *Entourage*. The main character, Vincent Chase, is a hot, successful, up-and-coming movie star who travels with a pack of close friends—Eric, Turtle, and his brother, Johnny Drama. Together, they make up the "entourage."

This show is obviously aimed at the young male demographic, but for me, as a woman, it still provides some good laughs from time to time. That said, I certainly didn't think I was going to find a beautiful example from this show for my work on presentations, but I did. In Episode 12 of Season 3, Vince is contemplating firing his agent and longtime supporter and friend, Ari Gold. On the advice of his brother, "Drama," Vince decides to explore several other talent agencies in Los Angeles before giving Ari the boot.

After a clearly unscientific selection process, Vince and his best friend and manager, Eric, head out to meet with the first agency. They walk into the slick Hollywood office and are quickly escorted to the conference room and seated at a large table with approximately twenty agents who are all representing the firm. The lead presenter stands up and says: "The way we see it, you are not just an actor, not just a movie star. You, sir, are a BRAND!"

A PowerPoint presentation flashes slides of the Mercedes Benz and Coca-Cola logos.

"Two of the most recognized names on the planet . . ." the presenter says.

Next is a head shot of . . . "Vincent Chase!"

"We intend to make you as popular as both of them!"

Now, after this first presentation, Vince and Eric are quite impressed and interested—until they get to the next agency.

They walk into another slick Hollywood office, and after some blatant schmoozing on the part of the lead presenter, they are escorted to the conference room. There they sit at a large table with another crew of approximately twenty agents all representing the firm. The lead presenter stands up and says: "The way we see it you are not just an actor. You, sir, are a BRAND!"

A PowerPoint presentation flashes slides of the Apple and Canon logos.

"Two of the most recognized names on the planet . . ." the presenter says.

Next is a head shot of . . . "Vincent Chase!"

"We intend to make you as popular as both of them!"

This time Vince and Eric come to the realization that the "big agencies are all cookie-cutter versions of each other." It's the same old, same old. They all claim to be different, but they are the same. So Vince and his pals start questioning the decision to leave Ari. After all, he is their friend and has been with them for a long time. They decide they'll stay where they are.

Meanwhile, Ari has heard through the industry grapevine that Vince has been visiting with other agencies. Upset and nearly traumatized, he decides to put forth a big effort to show Vince and Eric that he's the best. He invites them to his office for a meeting and, well, disaster ensues.

Vince and Eric walk into Ari's slick Hollywood office and are escorted to the conference room and seated at a large table with approximately twenty agents all representing the firm. Ari stands up and says, "The way we see it, you, Vince, are a BRAND!"

A PowerPoint presentation flashes slides of the Microsoft and McDonald's logos.

"Two of the most recognized names on the planet . . ." Ari says.

Next is a head shot of . . . "Vincent Chase!"

"We intend to make you as popular as both of them!"

Seeing this again—but this time from Ari—was a huge disappointment to Vince and Eric. They believed he was different and were shocked to find him using the same cookie-cutter presentation as everyone else. They get up from their seats and after a brief conversation, Eric says, "Ari, you're fired."

Doing the same things everyone else is doing but just changing a few words around does not dazzle your prospect. It's normal to want to copy a wonderful example, but I'd rather you use it as an inspiration to further develop your own material. To truly craft a creative message, you have to dig in and work at it, employing all kinds of your own stories, anecdotes, humor, and thought-provoking illustrations to keep your message fresh, unique, and different.

SKELETON VS. SOUL

If you liken the elevator speech to the human body, it's easy to see the structure of the persuasive case as the bones or the skeleton. In this chapter, we are creating the soul of your presentation, the piece that has the best chance of touching the heart and mind of your listener. As the soul links the human body to the world around it, the creative bridge we will build connects a logical, persuasive case to an authentic delivery.

Speech Supports

First, consider the speech support. The goal of your support materials is to link your argument to examples and illustrations that make the point easy to understand. Speech supports have the power to boost your credibility and rein in your prospect's attention.

One of the most effective speech supports is the anecdote or story. Most often, it's a short, engaging tale that makes your point in an entertaining way. Other popular and useful speech supports include:

1. **Analogy**—A similarity between like features of two things, on which a comparison may be based. "A good public relations department is to a real estate agency as fuel is to a jet."

2. **Definition**—The formal statement of the meaning or significance of a word, phrase, etc. "A speech, as defined by *Webster's*, is the practice of oral communication."

3. **Statistics**—The "collection, analysis, interpretation, and presentation" of huge quantities of numerical facts or data. "A recent survey suggests that adults actually remember 50 percent of what they hear in an oral presentation."

4. **Testimonials**—A declaration certifying the value or excellence, etc., of a thing. "The *New York Times* named Bob the most reliable, consistent businessman in history."

5. **Hypothesis**—A proposition set forth as an explanation for the occurrence of an event or trend. "Your company's recent slump in ad sales may be due to a lack of energy and inspiration in your print and online teams."

Rhetorical Devices

Second, consider the rhetorical device, a technique a speaker uses to evoke an emotional response. This tool is versatile and has the ability to enhance any presentation. Let's take a look at a couple of rhetorical devices:

> **Alliteration** is the excessive repetition of the sound of a particular letter within a sentence. "A bright, bilingual broker is just what your company needs to boost its bottom line!"

Anaphora; emphasizing words by repeating them at the beginning of neighboring clauses, was a device employed by Sen. Barack Obama often, and with great success, during the 2008 presidential campaign. For example, when he said, "Yes we can!" and "Not this time!" over and over, it engaged the audience and encouraged people to join in, repeating each phrase at just the appropriate time in cadence with the speaker. As the message progressed, Obama created a sense of unity between himself and the audience.

Other rhetorical devices include:

1. **Antithesis**—The use of contrasting words or phrases.

2. **Personification**—Giving human qualities to an inanimate object.

3. **Rhetorical question**—A question to which an answer is not expected in response.

4. **Aposiopesis**—The act of leaving a thought incomplete, usually through the sudden breaking off in speech, as in "Why, you little—!"

5. **Metaphor**—The use of a word or phrase to stand for another word or phrase on the basis of some similarity between the two.

Now that you have your tools in hand, it's time to discuss where you can find your best material. I've found it usually requires you to do a little creative research. Start collecting stories, magazine articles, and funny and compelling quotes. Put them into what I like to call a "File of Creative Examples" for ongoing use. To keep it packed with material, surf the Internet, search LexisNexis, cruise the bookstores, read newspapers, journals, and magazines, and listen to interesting speakers.

Always be on the lookout for examples that really hit home for you. And, of course, examine your own experiences. Some of the best material comes from your personal, academic, and professional lives. Remember, there's some validity to sayings such as, "You can't make this stuff up!" and "Truth is stranger than fiction!" and "The story you are about to hear is real, but the names have been changed to protect the innocent." So roll up your shirtsleeves and commit an hour or two a week to filling up your own File of Creative Examples.

CREATIVE WAYS TO OPEN YOUR PRESENTATIONS

An especially effective way to grab someone's attention is with a clever opening. It's a good idea to incorporate examples that are artistic, colorful, intuitive, and fun, as well as those that are linear, rational, and fact-based. Let me share some examples of people who have opened their talks in creative ways.

One simple and humorous method I have always admired is that of a gentleman named Tom Bayer, who was affiliated with a major mortgage banking company. He began his presentation by saying: "Hi, I'm Tom Bayer, as in Bayer Aspirin. I am not related to that Bayer family, but I *am* the lender who takes the headache out of the lending process." He then gracefully transitioned into the body of the talk, explaining how he would eliminate various "headaches" that might come up in the lending process.

It is equally important to use examples that are more analytical in nature; in other words, to get creatively persuasive with the hard, cold facts. A wonderful example of such an opening is found in President Harry S. Truman's famed "Whistle Stop Speech," given on September 18, 1948, in Chariton, Iowa (available from the University of Virginia, millercenter.org/Scripps/archive/speeches/detail/3348). During that speech, "Give 'Em Hell" Harry used numbers and statistics to open his audience's eyes to what the opposition was doing. Here's some of what he told folks that day:

"In 1932, 123,000 farmers in the United States had lost their farms. In 1947, less than 800 farms were foreclosed. That's the greatest record in history.

"In 1932, the farmers were hopelessly in debt. Their indebtedness has been reduced by more than 50 percent and they have $18 billion in assets. Think of that! Just think of that!"

Truman went on to warn his audience that the Republicans wanted to reverse that prosperity, do away with price-support programs for farmers, and "turn the clock back to the horse-and-buggy days with such people that made up the 'do-nothing' 80th Congress."

He then placed the solution to the problem—whether to progress or not—squarely in the hands of his audience:

"That Congress tried its level best to take all the rights away from labor . . . to put the farmer back to 1932 . . . to put small business out of business . . . You stayed at home in 1946, and you got the 80th Congress, and you got just exactly what you deserved. You didn't exercise your God-given right to control this country. Now you're going to have another chance. If you let that chance slip, you won't have my sympathy. If you don't let that chance slip, you'll do me a very great favor, for I'll live in the White House another 4 years."

And he did.

Truman was reelected President of the United States on November 2, 1948. Granted, he was the sitting president, and we can't all be as aggressive as Harry S. Truman was that day, but we can take a cue from his passion and certainty and, of course, his use of numbers and statistics. (For more inspiring examples of great speeches, I recommend you read Michael Waldman's *My Fellow Americans: The Most Important Speeches of America's Presidents, from George Washington to George W. Bush* [Naperville, IL: Sourcebooks Inc., 2003].)

Here's an example from the softer side. I remember a young woman who was really shy and uncertain about delivering her presentation. She walked to the front of the conference room, greeted the audience, and launched into a story she'd heard often during her childhood.

It went something like this: In a tiny corner of a big house, Mama Mouse sat with her Baby Mouse. The two were very hungry but could find no food. As they scurried to the kitchen to keep searching, they spotted a giant piece of cheese. But the largest and meanest cat in the big house sat sleeping near the cheese.

"Mama, I'm so hungry!" said Baby Mouse. "How will we ever get to the cheese?"

"Not to worry," said Mama Mouse. "I have an idea!"

Suddenly, Mama Mouse began barking like a dog at the top of her lungs. "Woof, woof, woof, grrrrowwl!" The large, mean cat woke up with a screech and raced out the door. Mama Mouse and Baby Mouse pounced on the cheese with joy.

Now at this point, I was thinking, *Yikes! Where is she going with this?* and suddenly, she hits the big line.

"See, junior," said Mama Mouse, "I always told you it pays to be bilingual!"

The woman then explained how important it was to partner

with a sales professional who is bilingual in today's market. By the end of the woman's talk, it became clear that her story was a unique way of showcasing one of her unique selling points—the ability to speak more than one language. The group loved her.

Here's a final example of a creative opening. I was working with a client, a woman named Jeremy Kelly. She needed a clever yet brief opening for her three-minute elevator speech that addressed the common perception that all home warranty companies are the same. The following is what we came up with:

"Big Foot, the Loch Ness Monster, and the Abominable Snowman," Jeremy said to her audience. "What do these characters all have in common? They are all urban legends. Here's another urban legend that impacts everyone in this room. It's the myth that all home warranty companies are the same.

"Hi, I'm Jeremy Kelly, and during the next few minutes, I am going to do my best to dispel this myth," she continued. "I will show you what separates me from my competitors and share why top producers like you choose to partner with our company in today's market."

Jeremy's opening was creative, succinct, and set up the rest of her talk for the next three minutes. She used the urban legends theme sparingly, when appropriate, and in her close she nicely tied everything together. The audience was interested and engaged and ultimately responded well to her message.

These examples illustrate how people have used speech supports and rhetorical devices to open their elevator speeches and carry their messaging theme throughout the entire presentation, which helps to tie the points together. In an elevator speech you synthesize a great deal of information, and a thematic package can help you make your message far more manageable for you and your audience to absorb.

USING CREATIVITY IN THE BODY OF YOUR PRESENTATION

Sometimes creativity simply means being unique. For instance, maybe you decide to include a refreshing dose of professional honesty in your presentation. Try telling a "How I Saved the Day" story. Paint a picture of why your company's customer service is, indeed, better than the competition's. Such a story is a different way of acknowledging the concerns your prospects may have and offering them a proven solution. Such a story also passes the "So what?" test we discussed in Chapter 5. You've presented your selling points but moved beyond the general into the specific.

It's essential that in the midst of all this creativity you bridge the gap between what you mean and what your listener understands. You might know what you mean and what you want to say, but getting that message out of your head, past your lips, and into the mind of someone else is the challenge of every creative speaker. So dig in and be clear and fresh without going over the top.

GETTING CREATIVE WITH YOUR CLOSE

Closing a presentation is essential. Closing with creativity is genius. It's also called bookending, that is, opening and closing your talk with the same creative tie-in. Recall Tom Bayer, who vowed to be the lender who "takes the headache out of the lending process." When wrapping up, Tom staples a sample packet of Bayer Aspirin to his business card and then reminds his audience he's there to ease their lending headaches literally and figuratively. He follows up his claim with specific ways that he works to relieve the borrowers' stress and reasons why they should do business with him. Tom leaves his listeners with the distinct feeling that he has tried especially hard to earn their business. And people remember his name.

Another way to close is by directly engaging your audience. Let's say Lisa, a developer, is promoting a new planned coastal community to a group of local real estate agents. At the end of her talk, Lisa holds up a bottle of champagne and passes around a giant fishbowl. "I am going to give away this bottle of Dom Perignon today!" she announces to the audience. "All you have to do is take out a business card and write down on the back the best time for me to follow up with you. I look forward to visiting with you and telling you more about these properties. Hopefully, we can celebrate a closed transaction together!"

The business card drawing is a simple, straightforward method of trying to set up appointments at the end of a three-minute elevator speech in front of a group. Giving away a bottle of champagne, nonalcoholic if necessary, may or may not be legal or appropriate in your market, so be sure to follow appropriate policies and tailor this concept to your own prospects.

At this point, you've engaged and enticed your listener or listeners in a creative and mildly clever way. They are bound to remember your talk, and everyone wants a chance at winning a nice prize.

PROCEED WITH CAUTION

Admittedly, some of these illustrations might be a little showy or campy. While going over the top can work for some people in some situations, when it comes to public speaking, my personal feeling is that subtle is better. Or, to put it another way: If you know you have the gumption to pull it off, go for it. If you're the least bit uncertain, it's probably smarter to tone it down. For example, I am reminded of a woman who "wowed" her audience by starting her inner office presentation with a rousing rendition of Aretha Franklin's "Respect." She had a great voice, and it really woke people up and got them smiling. Her rather bold method worked with that group because she had a great voice and her audience knew her and liked her.

I am also reminded of a woman who used the same method but missed the mark because she did not have a great voice or the confidence to pull it off. Ultimately, the singing attempt was a flop and, unfortunately, her message was overshadowed and her presentation was memorable in all of the wrong ways.

Don't Get Too Cheesy

I personally do not like it when a presenter gets too kitschy. But, ultimately, everyone has to chart his or her own path. Here are two examples of presentations that have the potential to get cheesy, but they just might work depending on the audience and the skills of the speaker.

I once heard a former naval aviator give a presentation in which he discussed all the qualities it takes to be a Top Gun pilot. Using aviator language and weaving in the excitement of the Top Gun experience, he explained that those same qualities are what make him a good businessman. While being a top-notch pilot is truly a unique life experience, relying on such a theme for an elevator speech is a little risky. It worked for him because he had the presence and the credibility to pull it off, but it might not work for someone else who doesn't have comparable experience and style or who is not a legitimate Top Gun pilot in real life.

Another example involves a woman who was unprepared and tried to pull off creativity at the last minute while attending a conference in Orlando. The night before the talk, she found herself without a plan and decided to wing it. She ran down to a Disney gift shop in the lobby, bought a magic wand, and decided to use that to make her point. The presentation was confusing and disjointed, and no one really knew what she was trying to say or what the magic wand had to do with her presentation. Waving a wand around might have seemed like a good way to grab attention and be creative at the last minute while in Florida, but in reality, it failed miserably. The theme and the content had no connection.

NOTE: If you want to use a creative theme, make sure the theme and the content of your points tie together. Don't use a theme just for the sake of attempting to be creative. It must clearly provide unity to the message as a whole.

Think carefully. If you feel like you're straying into potentially dangerous territory, step back and make sure you are communicating a message that your audience can relate to and find relevant. Remember, you're trying to be credible and memorable, so don't let your creativity end up being an off-putting distraction from your message. Your goal is to increase your credibility, not undermine it.

PERSPECTIVE IS EVERYTHING

We can say that Bill Cosby, Ellen DeGeneres, Eddie Murphy, Tina Fey, Amy Poehler, and Jerry Seinfeld are great comedians. They are creative and funny people, but it's not just what they say. It's how they say it as well. They all have their own unique way of looking at the world. To close this chapter, let's consider the perspective they bring to their message. In the next chapter, we will examine their authentic delivery.

No one can match the subtle, comic observations of Bill Cosby or the outrageous musings of Jerry Seinfeld. Each man has a unique and truly clever perspective. So it makes sense to suggest that one way of stepping into a space of creativity is to look through someone else's eyes. Change your vantage point. Listen to your presentation through the ears of your grandmother or your sixteen-year-old nephew or your husband or wife. Try to play the role of listener as you read over and look at your three-minute elevator speech.

In summary, remember that creativity is the second benchmark in developing a successful presentation. Imagine how you can bookend your next talk, weaving in fabulous creative ideas to illustrate your point and then imagine what it's like to be the listener hearing your message.

NEXT

We will delve into the third benchmark, authentic delivery, and each of us will learn how to speak in our own unique voice.

REVIEW
GET CREATIVE AND BRING
THE MESSAGE TO LIFE

❖ The second benchmark is creativity. Stories, anecdotes, humor, and examples help you touch the hearts and minds of your listeners.

❖ Doing the same things everyone else is doing or just changing a few words around is not creativity. It's imitation. To truly craft a creative message, you have to dig in and work at it, employing your own stories, anecdotes, humor, and thought-provoking illustrations to keep your message fresh, unique, and different.

❖ Speech supports and rhetorical devices are wonderful tools to use when crafting a creative and engaging presentation.

❖ Don't get cheesy. Think carefully before you stray into potentially dangerous territory. Step back and make sure you are delivering a speech that your audience can relate to and find relevant. Don't let your creativity end up being an off-putting distraction from your message.

❖ Change your vantage point. Listen to your presentation through the ears of your grandmother or your sixteen-year-old nephew or your husband or wife. Try to play the role of listener as you read over and look at your three-minute elevator speech.

seven

Delivery: Speak in Your Own Authentic Voice

I have noticed through the years that there's something about actually delivering a presentation that absolutely terrifies many of my clients. Most of them are fine with speaking in front of strangers, but put them in a room with their peers or those who really know their business, and they struggle with it tremendously. They worry so much about how the presentation will sound that they are distracted from the real task—landing their message. Delivery, the moment we tie our case and our creativity to an actual performance, is the third benchmark by which we measure a great presentation.

In the previous chapter, we talked about creativity and the importance of gathering all kinds of different stories and anecdotes to bring the message to life in our presentations. For years I have been gathering examples and story nuggets that help to illustrate different points. The following story has been tucked away in my mental filing cabinet waiting for just the right moment to help me create a beautiful example of the significance of the marriage of creativity and delivery in our presentations.

IT'S THE PRESENTER'S JOB TO BRING THE MESSAGE TO LIFE

I love the 1996 film *The Mirror Has Two Faces*, starring Barbra Streisand as Rose Morgan and Jeff Bridges as Gregory Larkin. It's a wonderful, rich, and clever film about two people who agree to an unconventional relationship, get married, and then ultimately fall in love. I admit that it falls into the chick-flick category. However, nestled inside this layered tale of dating and real love is a great little sub-story that has nothing to do with the romantic tale. So, for all the guys reading this book, don't worry; you don't need to skip over this part. In fact, you might really like it.

Both Rose and Gregory teach at Columbia University. She's a professor of literature, and he's a professor of calculus. The two have never met, and they are about to be set up on a date. Gregory places a personal ad that is answered by Rose's sister on her behalf and without Rose's knowledge. He decides he wants to see what Rose is like before they go out, so he pops in on one of her lectures. As Gregory sits down in the class with the rest of the 100-plus students in attendance, he sees Rose leading the class in an engaging presentation with lots of juicy material and fantastic style. She clearly has an incredible connection with the audience. They love her! She is real and raw and speaking beautifully in her own voice.

Not surprisingly, Rose checks up on Gregory too. He's leading a course on some calculus principle: his tone is that of a boring mathematics professor, and some of his students are falling asleep, while others are trying to sneak out. But Gregory is nice looking and Rose hasn't had that many dates, so when he catches her in the act of sneaking a peek at him, they confirm the date.

Somewhere during that first date, Gregory mentions to Rose that he dropped by her class, compliments her teaching style, and asks, "How do you get them to stay?"

On the second date he asks if she will come by one of his classes.

On the next visit she gives him her feedback.

"You need to relate to your students," Rose tells Gregory. "Your back is to the class, and it seems as if you are having a 'math party' and you only invited yourself."

She suggests that he needs to relax and have fun, tell a story, maybe put some humor into it. (Gosh, is this sounding familiar!) The movie then transitions to the future: Gregory and Rose continue to date and shortly thereafter they are married.

Rose is a baseball fan, and one day while watching a game Gregory says, "I've never understood people's fascination with baseball."

"Really?" she says. "Actually, the game should really interest you as it is all about stats and averages." She then proceeds to explain the game from a mathematical perspective.

Flash forward to Gregory's next day in class, and the scene is typical. He's droning on, students are slipping into a state of boredom, and then he stops and says: "Anybody see the game yesterday? Let me see if I can put this another way." He then uses the personal story about watching baseball with his wife and creates a bridge into how hitting a home run relates to measuring trajectory and velocity. Suddenly, his audience is awake. He's facing them. His style is coming to life, and his students are engaged in his lecture. Gregory is thrilled!

When he gets home, he tells Rose what happened and exclaims: "I could not believe it. Suddenly the room was filled with tangible energy . . . We were connected . . . and they stayed!"

Gregory goes on to thank her profusely and says, "I was a better teacher today than I have ever been before, because of you." Nice!

So, What Does This Illustration Show Us?

This is such an incredible awakening for Gregory, and he releases his old-school, arrogant "professor speak" and becomes himself. Speaking in his own authentic voice and creating a real-life example the audience can relate to, he is able to make his calculus material so much more engaging!

I love this illustration. It shows how a reluctant math teacher learns that he doesn't have to be boring just because he thinks his core material is boring. It shows how it's always the presenter's job to bring the material to life. It shows how using a personal illustration and anecdote in messaging can help someone find his or her own authentic voice and how the audience will respond immediately when you're speaking *with* them, not *at* them. It also shows how much more fun you, as a presenter, will have sharing your material when you connect with the audience and generate positive responses from your listener.

This is why authentic delivery is the third benchmark. The persuasive case is very important because it is the foundation of your presentation. The creativity in your message helps reach the hearts and minds of your listeners. The delivery sets the tone and helps the listener hear you, your spirit, and experience a sincere connection.

YOU ARE THE STORYTELLER

To help people reach the third benchmark of delivery, I often remind them it's not just what you say, but how you say it. In our training workshops, one particularly helpful exercise asks participants to deliver a three-minute adventure story with a moral. Each person is granted the freedom to make a presentation with his or her own style, flair, and humor. In many cases, I get the look of terror or the protest "That's just not me!" or the response "I'm not like that!" But after they give it a try, these same people are often amazed at what they have accomplished. During the three-minute adventure story, their message comes to life and they are animated and interesting. They are able to shed the buttoned-down professional persona and show the audience who they really are.

Maybe they share a story about the day they went skydiving or swimming with dolphins or hiking up a beautiful hill. Maybe Bob tells about the day he asked his girlfriend to be his wife or the wild ride to the hospital the night she went into labor or how they once ran into a bear on a camping trip or the time they survived a storm on a sailboat. Whatever the tale, men and women of all ages and from all walks of life become engaging storytellers when they move beyond the old "Stepford" mechanical business mode and rediscover how to be real, human presenters.

At this point I want to remind you that the more you speak from your heart and personal experiences, the deeper the connection will be that you form with the audience. As your personality and style shine through, your talk will unfold in the mind of the listener. When you're sure of your subject, you're more relaxed and sincere. Polish might come from practice, but charisma—the trait that draws an audience closer—comes from certainty. It's owning the message and sharing it with your personal conviction and perspective.

It's difficult to provide you with exact guidelines because delivery is such a personal and subjective skill. What works for one person simply may not work for anyone else. I do, however, have a few suggestions:

1. **Rev it up.** A little energy and enthusiasm go a long way when you're trying to engage an audience. You want the talk to be enjoyable, so give yourself permission to have a little fun. Display confidence and an authentic presence by speaking in a personal voice. Remember the importance of using a full range of expression and emphasis. Your talk will include highs and lows—everything from lighthearted punch lines to dramatic pauses—and, much like an actor does, you must adjust your rate and tone accordingly.

2. **Find the right word.** Using good diction and a comprehensive vocabulary is not magic. It takes effort and the willingness to dig into a dictionary or thesaurus, either in print or online, and try out new words. I still recommend *30 Days to a More Powerful Vocabulary* by Wilfred Funk (New York: Simon & Schuster, 2003) to my clients to help them explore a more colorful way to describe elements within their talks. It's worth the time because finding the perfect word is a great feeling.

3. **Move with meaning.** It helps to have a grace and flow to your physical movements as you present your talks. You will want to have an awareness of your body language and

avoid distracting gestures. Clenched hands, flailing arms, and dancing feet are a great way to detract from your elevator speech. Trained competitors in speech and debate in high school and in college are taught to make their movements natural yet still meaningful during a presentation.

One useful tool I recommend is the Six Point Star method (see diagram that follows) that I developed for Sjodin Communications. It is an exercise that teaches you how to align your stance and movement with the six components of your elevator speech. (This diagram is also available in the free downloads section at www.smallmessagebigimpact.com.)

- ❖ Start in the center of the room and make your introduction; this is Position 1.

- ❖ Take two or three small steps slightly to the right, plant your feet, and deliver your first body point; this is Position 2.

- ❖ Walk three or four steps back to the center, plant your feet, and make the second body point of your presentation; this is Position 3.

- ❖ Continue three or four more steps to the left, plant your feet, and make the third body point of your presentation; this is Position 4.

- ❖ Walk slightly ahead and back toward the center of the room, plant your feet, and start your conclusion; this is Position 5.

- ❖ Take one or two steps forward, plant your feet, and make your close; this is Position 6.

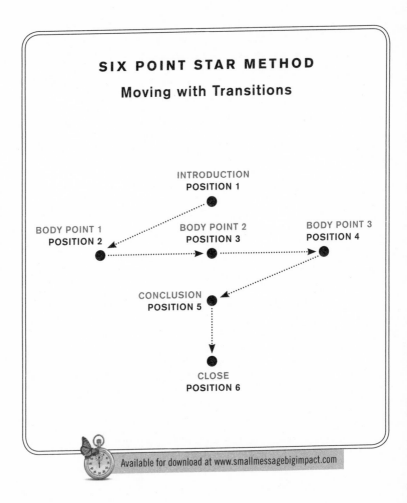

The Six Point Star method provides nonverbal cues to the audience that you are transitioning from one idea or concept to another. It helps you, as the presenter, stay on track with your talk and keep your story moving progressively forward. Give it a try.

NOTE: Of course, the Six Point Star method applies when you are making a group presentation. You would look pretty silly if you did this in someone's cramped office or in the middle of a cocktail party.

4. **Use visual aids effectively.** Remember, you are the star and visual aids are only a bit player, especially in a three-minute elevator speech. Whether your visual aids are high tech or low tech, keep them simple and easy to understand. Most scenarios are going to be spontaneous, and you won't have the luxury of visual aids. Always ask yourself, "Is this visual aid appropriate for the length of the talk?"

5. **Dress appropriately.** Make sure you are wearing an outfit suitable for the type of meeting you are attending. Get to know the culture from which your audience will be drawn. Dress as though you are aware of current fashion trends, but don't overdo it. Sometimes people approach me in private and say, "Hey, Terri, I agree with you on dressing up to show honor and respect for your clients' time, but I don't have a ton of money to spend on designer clothes!"

At this point, I share with them a little pearl of wisdom about appropriate dress I learned from my Nana and Pop-Pops, both British, polite, elegant people. He was a tailor for J.C. Penney and she was a secretary for Kaiser. They were not affluent, but they were the classiest people I have ever known, always neatly laundered, pressed, and put together. My grandparents taught me that class has nothing to do with having money. Dressing appropriately can be done on a limited budget as long as you have a couple of conservative items that you can get tailored to fit nicely. It is possible to look sharp and professional without going into debt. What is most important is that you look clean, polished, and pressed to show honor and respect for your clients and prospects. When you're dressed up, you carry yourself differently. There's something about being dressed for "game day" that puts a finishing touch on your presentation.

FIND YOUR VOICE

In Chapter 6, I broached the subject of the unique creativity of successful comedians Bill Cosby, Ellen DeGeneres, Eddie Murphy, Tina Fey, Amy Poehler, and Jerry Seinfeld. Now let's pause for a moment and think of how different they all are in terms of style. They all have incredible delivery, yet there's almost nothing the same about them. They all understand how to build a great comedy piece and use their own brand of creativity, but even more important, they all speak in their own voice. They have their own presenting styles and allow their distinct personalities to shine through.

Have you ever been to a comedy show and laughed until you were almost in tears? Have you ever gone home and then tried to retell the jokes you heard at the comedy show the night before? It never seems to be as funny as when the comedian who created it shared it, does it?

No.

Why not? For many reasons, including timing, delivery, and practice. Most important, however, is that it's their story. No one else can share their story the way they can. And no one can share your elevator speech the way you can! It's your message, told in your voice. Remember, there is an art to presenting, and that art takes place in your delivery.

FACE THE FEAR

It's at this point in our workshops that many people become worried and start to falter a bit. To put it simply, they freak out! And I get it. They are overwhelmed, struggling to remember and incorporate everything they just learned. They have their lists, their examples, their body points, and even their fidgeting under control, but when the time comes to actually stand up and start speaking, they have trouble pulling it all together the first time they try. And that's okay. It's normal! Breathe. Practice. It takes a little time. I understand that your fear can be paralyzing, and I don't dismiss it lightly. In fact, I can offer you some perspective.

First, acknowledge that the fear is real and a normal occurrence for people working on developing this skill. Human beings, even high achievers, get scared of the unknown. Second, see those nerves for what they actually are—a lesson. The minute you become nervous, you are standing in a space of learning. You are about to learn something you did not know before. You are about to learn how to drive through the fear to the other side. Learning puts you back in the space of seeing things from a fresh perspective. Remember the saying: "When you're green, you're growing. When you're ripe, you're rotting." It's good to be green!

I find it helpful to anticipate what I will feel like on the other side, that space of completion, invigoration, and accomplishment. Sure, the weight of the outcome of a presentation can jangle your nerves and stop you in your tracks, but what if you gave in to the fear? What if you never took that step? Nothing would ever change. And if you don't try, then the cause-and-effect benefits and the magic of the Elevator Speech Effect cannot work for you. It's like the slogan for the California state lottery: "You can't win if you don't play!" Remember, it's not how nervous you are that counts; it's how you push through the fear and execute your presentation.

So, what is the solution? There is only one, and that is practice, practice, practice. Here's one of the best truths I can possibly share with you: at the end of the day, your elevator speech doesn't have to be 100 percent perfect to work. I promise! So don't worry if it isn't perfect. Do your best, speak in your own authentic voice, and trust in the power of the Elevator Speech Effect.

NEXT

Get ready to take your carefully crafted message out into the real world and earn the opportunity to be heard.

REVIEW

DELIVERY: SPEAK IN YOUR OWN AUTHENTIC VOICE

❖ Delivery, the moment we tie our case and creativity to an actual performance, is the third benchmark by which we measure a great presentation.

❖ You are the storyteller. Polish comes from practice, but charisma comes from certainty.

❖ Share your message from your authentic voice.

❖ Find the right word. Use good diction and a comprehensive vocabulary to enhance your presentation. It takes effort and the willingness to dig into a dictionary or thesaurus, either in print or online, and try out new words.

❖ Move with meaning. Avoid distracting body language. Clenched hands, flailing arms, and dancing feet are a great way to detract from your own talk. Use our proven Six Point Star method to keep your presentation on track.

❖ Dress appropriately. Make sure you are wearing an outfit suitable for the type of meeting you are attending. Get to know the culture from which your audience will be drawn. Dress up to show honor and respect for your clients and prospects.

❖ Face your fear and acknowledge that it is real and normal. Everyone gets scared of the unknown. See those nerves for what they actually are—a lesson. Realize you are about to learn something you did not know before.

eight

Earn the Right to Be Heard

Consider once again the Butterfly Effect—that notion put forth by MIT meteorologist Edward Lorenz that a massive storm might have its roots in the faraway flapping of a tiny butterfly's wings. Of course, the concept cannot be proven, but it also cannot be disproven. So why not apply it to the practice of elevator speeches? Assume that one, tiny presentation at the outset of your journey could ultimately result in the fruition of your short- and long-term plans—and the magic of the Elevator Speech Effect can begin to generate a positive ripple effect forward.

The motivation to put yourself out there and make something happen is derived from the potential to attain your goals and dreams. After drafting your talk, it's time to create opportunities to deliver it. Although it may feel intimidating at times, you must take action in order to make something happen strategically. You can wish, dream, hope, and pray, but as the old West African proverb suggests, "When you pray, move your feet."

BE A LITTLE SCRAPPY

Having read up to this point, you may be thinking, "OK, Terri, I have this elevator speech, but how do I get in the door to share it?" The answer is, sometimes you have to get a little scrappy. By scrappy I mean you must be willing to get out in front of your prospect and take some risks to land that longer appointment in the future. I like the *American Heritage Dictionary's* definition of scrappy: "full of fighting spirit." So get in there and fight the good fight. Stop waiting for that job or promotion or raise or next sale to simply drop out of the sky and into your lap. Apply your imagination and take creative risks to make things happen.

> "Logic will get you from A to B," he once said. "Imagination will take you everywhere."
> —Albert Einstein

Being scrappy is a commitment, of sorts, to stand up for yourself and speak up about your vision for your future despite the inherent risks of embarrassment, rejection, or even failure.

To earn the right to be heard, you often need to do a little extra homework and customize your approach in a way that is unrivaled. Is it possible to do some "intel" before you approach that person? This requires natural curiosity and active listening. Don't go for the typical kids and sports questions. That doesn't impress or dazzle to win. Instead, ask your prospect about his or her favorite authors, bands, hobbies, and movies. Can't talk directly to a prospect? Get the information from their friend, colleague, or administrative assistant. I'm talking about really rolling up your shirtsleeves and getting a little scrappy.

Using your imagination also helps keep your job fun, interesting, and fresh. Through the years, I have done lots of crazy little things to employ my scrappy effort, including sending a prospect a Pets.com puppet I learned she really wanted; finding a special Disney menorah; delivering organic cashews and green tea; obtaining signed books from favorite authors; special ordering a handmade vase from a young local artist; crafting unique embroidered pillows (not by me!); watching Bassmasters and learning about bass fishing; and even working free of charge to support someone else's effort.

I came across another great example when reading *Success* magazine, which profiled an amazingly scrappy effort by entrepreneur Donny Deutsch, owner of the Deutsch Inc., advertising agency and host of the hit CNBC television show *The Big Idea with Donny Deutsch*. Published in December 2008, the article described how, early in his career, Donny convinced his father not to sell David Deutsch Associates but instead to give Donny an expanded role in the company and the chance to create his own brand with new accounts.

Donny shared the story of one of his first big wins. He needed to capture the attention of the man in charge of awarding a huge advertising account for a regional car dealership. In a scrappy effort to earn the right to be heard, Donny got especially creative, shipping a variety of individual car parts to the decision maker, each one accompanied by a different message. For instance, the headlight said, "We'll Give You Bright Ideas," while the fender promised, "We'll Protect Your Rear End," and the steering wheel pledged, "We'll Steer You in the Right Direction."

He shipped one car part every half-hour for a twelve-hour period to the man's home. By the end of the day, Donny had sent twenty-four car parts and twenty-four unique and memorable messages.

Judy Alexandra DiEdwardo, in her article "The Age of the Entrepreneur" (*Success*, December 2008), summed it up this way: "The bold move was an instant hit with the client (he won the account!), and a poignant turning point for Deutsch, who had been struggling against convention to find his voice."

All of these creative approaches were designed to surprise and interest a difficult-to-reach prospect and to earn the right to be heard. While I hope you are starting to get a little jazzed about being scrappy, remember that your creativity might get you in the door, but you need to have a rock-solid presentation to deliver once you're inside to carry the transaction to completion. Try to think of your scrappy efforts as a progression of steps:

Step 1—Identify your most desirable target.

Step 2—Do homework to customize your approach.

Step 3—Employ your creative, scrappy strategy to gain the listener's attention.

Step 4—Deliver your well-crafted, persuasive elevator speech.

Step 5—Have fun with it.

Step 6—Speak in your own voice and you're there.

Step 7—Rinse and repeat.

It's easier if you view this entire endeavor as an organic process. Feel your way through these seven steps. Not every step applies to every situation.

REFERRALS AND ELEGANT INTRODUCTIONS

You might want to begin by simply identifying certain people who could help you line up referrals and elegant introductions. Sometimes you have to craft a solid little presentation through which you ask someone to help you by introducing you to someone else, and so on. Develop an awareness of the gentle nuances of a situation and adapt accordingly.

> "I am a success today because I had a friend who believed in me, and I didn't have the heart to let him down."
> — Abraham Lincoln

Referrals

A referral typically comes from someone who knows your work and has hired you or used your product or service and can provide testimony to validate your credibility.

I once crafted a mini-presentation to persuade a mentor of mine to refer me to one of his key contacts. The fact that he was my mentor and also a past client did not automatically land me an appointment with another person's company. This happens a lot: We have to give a presentation to get a presentation opportunity. The good news is that he agreed to give me the initial referral. This referral helped to get me past the gatekeeper, but then I was on my own.

Elegant Introductions

An introduction typically takes place between associates or friends who have not previously done business together. Let's say your friend Mark approaches you about needing the name of an intellectual property attorney. Let's assume you have not personally invented a new product or service for which you sought such an attorney, but nevertheless you know someone who specializes in that area and you are comfortable recommending him.

"Mark, my friend Jim is an intellectual property attorney. He is a smart guy and very talented. Even though I have not had to use his services personally, I do want to introduce the two of you because I think you might be of benefit to each other."

The introduction also can emphasize personal connections.

"Tom, this is Mary. Mary is a big fan of your work. She is a wonderful person. Mary works with individuals like you to accomplish these objectives: .... [fill in the blank]."

A graceful introduction is a kind and gentle way to set up visits without putting pressure on the individual who introduced you to endorse your work since they have not actually worked with you. If you are blessed to receive both a referral and an introduction from a previous client, the weight of such an endorsement is invaluable in helping you gain access to future prospects and contacts.

When asking an individual for either an introduction or a referral, keep in mind that they are helping you, and they have a right to say no without feeling pressured. They should be treated like gold, and you should respectfully earn their referral or introduction. If they seem uncomfortable, say: "No worries. Maybe this isn't a good time. If you feel it could be appropriate in the future, I would greatly appreciate it." Be gracious and leave like a lady or a gentleman.

When they say yes, rejoice and send a thank-you note, and treat the opportunity like the valuable asset and gift that it is!

NOTE: Don't be too pushy or presumptuous with the prospect. You have been given a graceful referral or introduction. You want to preserve the credibility of the person who recommended you.

Here's an example of someone who inappropriately handled a graceful introduction, which subsequently led to a series of problems.

An overzealous, top-producing financial services adviser—we'll call him Charles—was introduced to Susan through his client named Oscar, who was Susan's good friend. Oscar thought Susan would be open to hearing Charles' presentation based on his recommendation. A mishandled referral:

> **Problem 1**—Susan was a reluctant prospect, but she took the meeting because Oscar is her friend. The meeting with Charles happened only because she had trusted Oscar's referrals in the past.

> **Problem 2**—Charles was overly friendly with Susan from the start, taking a far too familiar approach in the initial meeting. The meeting also lasted too long, and though it ended respectfully, nothing ever came of it for Charles.

> **Problem 3**—Oscar then received a call from Susan, and she expressed her discomfort with the meeting with Charles. This ensured that Oscar would be less willing to give Charles a referral in the future.

> **Problem 4**—Charles burned the bridge he had with Oscar because he was too familiar and not respectful of the graceful introduction.

On the other hand, here's an example of a lovely way to employ a graceful introduction, namely, to set up a presentation to get a presentation appointment opportunity. It also shows how being a bit scrappy and following through on the process can work:

Set Up—Scrappy Sue is trying to expand her network and creates a list of new dream contacts. She asks a seasoned friend in the industry to look over her list to see if he might know anyone.

Next Step—Scrappy Sue's friend knows three people on the list and offers to make three phone calls for her. One person never responds, and two people are open-minded.

Next Step—Scrappy Sue follows up on the two leads she received. One person asks her to just send information, so she does and makes a note to follow up in a few days. The other person allowed the friend to give Scrappy Sue his contact information.

Next Step—Scrappy Sue asks for key intel about this new prospect, and the referring friend tells her that he does not know much about him except that he loves some "crazy Starbucks beverage."

Next Step—So, Scrappy Sue does a little research to find out which specific drink the prospect likes.

Next Step—She contacts the prospect, who is very busy, and she offers to bring his favorite beverage, a "Tazo Chai Tea Latte," for a quick visit at his office. He likes her scrappy approach and agrees to the appointment.

Next Step—Scrappy Sue shows up on time, looking sharp and with the designer tea in hand. She is invited into the office. The prospect thanks her for the tea and compliments her creative approach. She smiles and says, "I know you are really busy, and I truly appreciate your time, so I will make this brief." Scrappy Sue delivers her three-minute elevator speech and asks for a longer appointment in the future. The prospect smiles and says, "Wow that was a clever little speech!" He also calls out to his assistant and authorizes her to book a future appointment and to include two other people in on the presentation. Scrappy Sue is thrilled.

Next Step—When Scrappy Sue returns for that next appointment, she is prepared, has done her homework, and gives a thorough presentation. Afterward, a great deal of dialogue and follow-up occurs, and then, ultimately, after following her company's sales process, Scrappy Sue secures her first contract with this organization!

Final Step—She remembers to send a thank-you note to her friend, along with an invitation to a celebratory lunch! The client is thrilled, Scrappy Sue expanded her circle of influence, and everybody wins.

Being a little scrappy and inventive, plus employing a winning elevator speech, helped to bridge the gap between Scrappy Sue's initial introduction and the first visit with a prospect. This respectfully earned her the right to be heard at a later time. You can use the same process that Scrappy Sue did and give your audience a reason to sit up and say, "Hmm, this person might have something to say."

I hope that you will accept opportunities that come your way, and create opportunities of your own. Crafting a great talk is wonderful, but it isn't effective until you get it out of your head, across your lips, and into the ears and minds of an audience. None of that hard work will matter unless you can use it to actually generate the outcomes that you want.

LET'S GO!

You might be thinking: "This is all so creative. I could never do that!" Of course you can. Maybe you could start small like Scrappy Sue with the favorite-beverage approach, and as you get more comfortable you can move up to a more elaborate plan like Donny Deutsch used.

Or maybe you are saying to yourself: "This all makes sense if you own a business or you're in sales, but I'm not." "I'm an engineer." "I'm in human resources." "I'm in management." Why do I need to be scrappy? Why do I need to activate the Elevator Speech Effect?"

You might be surprised to learn that individuals who do not typically see themselves as salespeople—retail store managers, mechanical engineers, architects, human resource professionals—at times still have to present a case to senior management why they need more time, more money, and more resources. Why not employ a small but subtle scrappy strategy to help inspire your listeners to hear your proposition? You never know where it might lead!

Consider the young man who wanted to dazzle his boss in an attempt to position himself for a promotion in the future. He wanted to show his boss that he does his homework and will go the extra mile. Applying the scrappy strategy to his situation, he found out that his boss liked a certain author, who happened to be a friend of mine. To help my friend, I got the author to personalize a copy of his latest book. My friend was able to give the book to his boss, who was thrilled about the gift, which served as the bridge to my friend talking to him about the new position. Perfect! It's all about giving, and it doesn't have to send you into debt. Nothing I have ever done has been expensive, just creative. We are not trying to buy their business. We are trying to show people that we are authentically trying to connect with them and earn the right to be heard.

Sometimes it might take two or three approaches to land the best one. If you are scared, that's OK. You have to try. What's the worst thing that could happen?

"Twenty years from now you will be more disappointed by the things you didn't do than by the ones you did. So, throw off the bowlines. Sail away from the safe harbor. Catch the trade winds in your sails. Explore. Dream. Discover."
— Mark Twain

People

At this point I hope you are finding the inspiration to take your elevator speech to the streets, to employ your creativity and get a little scrappy. But maybe you are still struggling with crafting your list of prospects. Maybe you do not actually have any contacts because you are pursuing an entirely new area or maybe you are expanding into unknown territory. Perhaps you are embarking on a new journey and do not know where to start. Clearly, you have to start somewhere.

To realize the outcomes you desire, *your carefully crafted talk must make its way to the key players, the people who can directly or indirectly influence the opportunities you seek: the decision maker, the CEO, the agent, the angel investor, the purchasing manager, the recruiter, the donor, the buyer, the seller, and the star maker*. Start by doing some homework. Do you know someone who can help you? Who do you know who might know this person? How can you get just a few minutes to meet with this individual? No contacts? Start asking friends, family, and colleagues if they might know someone. Explore the possibility that you might be closer than you think to setting up at least one or two opportunities to connect with a key player who could put you on the right path. After all, it only takes one "yes." It might take meeting more than a hundred people, but it only takes one to open a door and say "yes!"

Pause for a moment and list the names of three people you know who may be able to introduce you or refer you to another contact that could help you move one step closer to your goal.

....

....

....

Places

Consider expanding beyond your friends, family, and current contacts. To stretch your boundaries, do some research in other areas. Show up and attend association meetings and conferences where individuals who have influence gather to network. Circulating in these venues will help you acquire new leads and contacts, and there are associations for all kinds of professions and fields these days.

For example, let's say you want to expand your business. Which groups and organizations in your backyard focus on your areas of interest or business demographic? Perhaps you want to write a book and have it published and you don't have a clue about getting a publisher. Why not attend Book Expo America to learn more about the industry and build contacts. Or maybe you want to develop a television show. Join the National Association of Television Program Executives, and you will find a wealth of opportunities to attend classes and conferences to expand your access as an independent television show producer.

Pause for a moment and make a list of association and industry places and meetings where you can network to help you acquire new leads and contacts.

....

....

....

Events

Another great way to put the spotlight on you, yourself, is to sponsor events with others or on your own. The event serves as the vehicle through which you introduce who you are and what your intentions are to expand your base of contacts. Many people won't realize they need you or your service, product, or idea until they attend the event and hear your elevator speech. And don't worry, options abound. You can host a party, buy a booth at a convention or trade show, or sponsor a hole at a golf tournament. You can even volunteer to work pro bono at an event to gain access to new and wonderful opportunities. Find the unique gatherings and meetings in your specific industry that few people know about. Dig, dig, dig.

Pause for a moment and list three events that you could attend or maybe even create to help develop more elevator speech opportunities for you and your company.

....

....

....

Now, with your lists in hand, you can begin taking action. You can launch your strategy to get a little scrappy and creatively take your elevator speeches to the streets!

Warning: No Stalking!

Remember, you are only going to dig as far as it's appropriate within the context of the professional relationship. If you go further than that, it's called stalking, and that's creepy. Do not focus on only one person, place, or opportunity. It's never a good idea to put all your eggs in one basket. There are many paths to getting to your desired outcome. Maintain a respectful approach and do not invade the personal privacy of your existing or potential contacts.

AUDIENCE ANALYSIS FOR GROUP PRESENTATIONS

Just as you did your homework to customize your three-minute elevator speech for a one-on-one talk, you will need to do a little analysis for a group presentation as well. So, consider using the Presentation Opportunity General Information Form, a copy of which follows in this chapter and is available as a free download at www.smallmessagebigimpact.com. Clearly, you can't use the same data for a one-on-one approach as you would for a group presentation, but you can still try to craft a clever attention-grabbing element that almost everyone in the audience can relate to, which will establish a foundation of general understanding.

This is just a start! Remember to define your intention: What is the goal of your group presentation? What do you want to happen? Just as you would with a one-on-one talk, you need to understand the demographics and basic backgrounds of the listeners in your group so that you can customize your presentation to grab their attention. Pause for a moment and ask yourself whether the audience will be made up mostly of Baby Boomers or Gen Xers or Millennials. Mostly men? Mostly women? Mostly entrepreneurs? A mixed group of all of the above?

Think about it this way. If you are touting the benefits of listening to music on an iPod, the musical references you use would differ depending on who is in your audience. More than likely, you would not reminisce about Elvis or the Rolling Stones with a group of Millennials. Nor would you laud the musical stylings of Lady Gaga or The Black Eyed Peas to a room full of Baby Boomers.

The data you can compile on this form is designed to guide you toward selecting timely information and illustrations that will better connect you to your listeners. Knowing your audience

PRESENTATION OPPORTUNITY
GENERAL INFORMATION FORM

I. WHAT IS THE GOAL OF YOUR PRESENTATION?

....

....

II. WHAT IS YOUR INTENTION?

....

....

III. AUDIENCE ANALYSIS INFORMATION

❖ Who are the listeners? ....

❖ Audience size? ....

❖ Average age of group? ....

❖ Male-female ratio? ....

❖ Attitude of audience? ....

❖ How informed is the audience? ....

IV. LOGISTICAL INFORMATION

❖ Facility ....

❖ Visual aid options ....

❖ Time allotted for presentation ....

❖ Who speaks before/after you ....

V. WHAT IS THE BEST WAY TO CLOSE IN THIS SITUATION?

....

....

is essential to providing them a well-crafted, customized talk that will entice them and make them more curious about you, your services, or your products and ideas.

READY TO LAUNCH

Whew! We have discussed getting scrappy, merged a lot of ideas, and explored several concepts toward earning the right to be heard. And at the end of the day, this is our basic road map to executing a winning elevator speech. I hope you are beginning to see the many different opportunities in which an elevator speech can be employed. I also hope you are beginning to wonder if there are other ways to use it. Are there still additional strategies to make an elevator speech work for you professionally, personally, and academically? The answer is a resounding "Yes!"

NEXT

Plus-ing the elevator speech is essential in this fast-paced world. We will review some creative approaches used by other individuals who have advanced their elevator speeches to an entirely new level.

REVIEW
EARN THE RIGHT TO BE HEARD

❖ Be a little scrappy. Apply your imagination and take creative risks to make things happen. Stop waiting for that job, promotion, raise, or next sale to simply drop into your lap. Be willing to get out in front of your prospect and take some risks to land that longer appointment time in the future. There is a progression of steps you can use to continually get in the door.

❖ Explore referrals and introductions to create opportunities.

❖ A referral typically comes from someone who knows your work and has hired you or used your product or service and can provide testimony to validate your credibility.

❖ An elegant introduction typically takes place between associates or friends who have not previously done business together.

❖ Knowing your audience is essential to providing them with a well-crafted, customized talk that will entice them and make them more curious about you, your services, or your products and ideas.

❖ We are trying to authentically connect with the audience.

❖ The Presentation Opportunity General Information Form will help you complete your initial audience analysis for presentations to a group.

nine

"Plus-ing" the Elevator Speech

Have you ever looked through a kaleidoscope? The slightest rotation and movement of the bits of glass at the bottom of the tube result in a continually shifting pattern of colors and shapes. All it takes is a small adjustment here or there and you have a dazzling montage of new possibilities. I believe the elevator speech can be just as dazzling when pushed or pulled in a different direction or used in a wide range of spaces.

Whether you are a business owner, a politician, or a commercial real estate executive, the scope of the usefulness of your speech is unlimited. By blending creativity, technology, and a sharp awareness of opportunity, you can successfully take your elevator speech to a new level.

In high school and in college, many of us played sports, sang in the chorus, worked on the yearbook committee, played in the marching band, ran track, performed with the drama club, or participated in some other group or activity. As I shared with you earlier, I was on the speech team.

I competed in Lincoln-Douglas policy debate and in individual events as well, including impromptu, extemporaneous, and persuasive speaking. Much of my time was spent practicing speeches, researching evidence to prove a case, and drafting briefs and notes, and I spent countless weekends at speech tournaments.

During those years, I learned the value of crafting a variety of different arguments to prove a point. I learned that it did not matter what you thought unless you could build a logical, persuasive argument with evidence to "prove" your case.

Ultimately, as a debater, you learn how to craft a variety of elevator speeches and use them individually or to combine several together to build a longer presentation when given the time. This training helped me to repurpose the arguments and content of my messages, or what I like to call plus-ing the elevator speech.

I recently learned from my friend John Fund that President Ronald Reagan employed this same strategy of preparing a variety of short talking points. Consider the following illustration. John Fund is an award-winning political writer for the *Wall Street Journal*. A number of times we have both been invited to speak at the same events, and I always enjoy hearing his stories and his perspective. Following one of his talks at a fund-raiser for Rep. John Campbell (R-CA) at the Balboa Bay Club in Newport Beach, California, we sat down to relax and visit for a bit. We started talking about my presentations on elevator speeches.

"Terri, your whole presentation on three-minute elevator speeches is really a spin on what Reagan used to do with his speeches," John said.

"Really? How's that?" I asked.

"Because Ronald Reagan basically had a three-minute elevator speech card for a variety of different subjects. I imagine he must have had one for everything from the Cold War to the economy and Social Security. There were times when you could literally see Reagan reach into his pocket and pull out index cards and slide them onto the podium. After looking them over and delivering his speech, he would subtly slide them back into his pocket.

"Depending on where he was going and who his audience was," John continued, "plus how much time he had to present, he would look over a small stack of cards and select the subject and issue cards that were most relevant and timely for that group.

"If he had other speeches in the same day, he could pick and choose new cards that would be relevant for that group. Then he would weave the new anecdotes and content together and that would become his next speech."

"I didn't know that!" I said.

"He was considered to be a very persuasive presenter because he always tailored his speeches to meet the needs of his audience and asked people to participate on some level," John added. "That's part of the reason he was called 'The Great Communicator.' And even today's political candidates, both Democrats and Republicans, regard him as one of the best presidential speakers in history."

What does this mean for you? On various days you might be meeting with or speaking to a wide range of decision makers, clients, and prospects. Why not create a collection of targeted elevator pitches for each of your propositions, arguments, ideas, products, and services? After all, what you want to say to a decision maker in technology will differ from what you might need or want to say to someone in human resources later on the same day. The case you would present to a potential investor would differ greatly from the case you would present to the end user of your services. And of course, someone who donates money to your philanthropic effort might need to hear a different case from the one you present to a corporation that might donate equipment or food to your cause.

You do not have to be the president of the United States to get people to listen to you. But you can communicate just as effectively as Ronald Reagan did by learning the art of using the elevator speech concept in a variety of ways. I hope you are now beginning to ponder different ways elevator speech content and material can be repurposed. Let's look at a couple of unique applications used by other individuals who have embraced this concept and taken it to a new level.

Additional Examples of Plus-ing the Elevator Speech

Bob Chesney of Chesney Communications has uploaded his three-and-a-half-minute elevator speech onto his company's website. His intention is to convert more of the prospects surfing the Internet to a higher percentage of live, potential leads.

When you get to the site, you notice that it has very few pictures and words; rather, it opens with Bob delivering an interesting elevator speech that highlights four ways to "Bring Your Marketing Strategy to the 21st Century." The viewer is then invited to click through various segments on the site for more specific information. Bob's speech explains how his company is a leader in video communications, and he shares three or four innovative ways he can help market your business. He closes with a clear call to action: "So pick up the phone and let's talk. To schedule a complimentary strategy session, please call us toll free at . . . We look forward to hearing from you!" This is about as specific as you can be when closing for the next appointment time via the Internet.

Even if Bob's site gets just a hundred hits each day, that is a quantum leap beyond what he himself can personally deliver. Plus, he is delivering his elevator speech while sleeping, working on other deals, and running errands during the day. Outstanding!

You can use this same strategy in plus-ing your elevator speeches. Take a second look at your web presence or television ads and see how creative you can be.

Here's another unique example. What started out as a traditional three-minute elevator speech has morphed into more. Sperry Van Ness hired Sjodin Communications to deliver our workshop on the three-minute elevator speech to a group of twenty of the company's "top producers." Approximately one year after that training, Jerry Anderson, CCIM, who owns the master license for Sperry Van Ness Commercial Real Estate for the state of Florida, decided to expand on the elevator speech training he received and take it to another level to build his organization's prospect base in a challenging market.

Jerry is a true believer in the power of today's new, morphed elevator speech concept and uses it to provide hundreds of agents around the state with a tool that consistently and effectively tells how his company differs from its competitors—to the benefit of the client:

> Terri, as you know, I believe that less is more. The best part of our new, morphed approach is what it can do before the agent even meets the prospect face-to-face. We converted our Sperry Van Ness Florida corporate elevator speech into what we now call a "2.5-minute media elevator pitch" that agents use to sell the Sperry Van Ness Commercial Real Estate Story online.

The prospect can start and stop or fast-forward at will, and yet the message is engaging, persuasive, and fast-paced. It is delivered consistently and accurately—something our agents don't always do when delivering in person, to say the least. (Believe me, we have tried for years to train everyone to understand and deliver the message, and some are always better than others.) So this has really helped to ensure the consistency and accuracy of our message. What our agents are good at is being their friendly, personal selves engaged in meaningful and probing interaction. This strategy plays to their strengths.

The result? A perfect illustration of the "Elevator Speech Effect." Our 2.5-minute media elevator pitch helps the sales force and has helped us as an organization to convert more leads to prospects.

In one example, Sperry Van Ness's two-and-a-half-minute media elevator pitch led to an appointment with a prospect who hired the company to market more than 10 million dollars' worth of commercial property. The meeting to close the deal lasted less than forty-five minutes.

"Without a short, fast-paced electronic elevator speech," Jerry concluded, "we might have bored the prospect with our old rendition and never have reached the most important person in the room—the prospect. Let me rephrase that—our client!"

IT WORKS!

College student, president of the United States, small business owners. They all applied the plus-ing the elevator speech strategy in different places, in different ways, and for different reasons. And it works! So, take a moment and think about ways of plus-ing your own three-minute elevator speech and allow the kaleidoscope of possibilities to unfold.

NEXT

We will craft a complete sample elevator speech outline for your review and to serve as a simple guide to help you build your next elevator speech.

REVIEW
"PLUS-ING" THE ELEVATOR SPEECH

❖ Craft a variety of elevator speeches or talking points and use them individually or combine several to build a longer presentation when given more time.

❖ Just like President Ronald Reagan, you can create a collection of targeted elevator pitches for each of your propositions, arguments, ideas, products and services, using small, convenient index cards.

❖ "Plus" your elevator speech by taking it to the Internet or radio or television. New platforms can produce opportunities, prospects, or sales.

❖ Think of alternative approaches to plus-ing the elevator speech in your market.

ten

Walk Through It Before You Run with It

"Don't wish it was easier; wish you were better.
Don't wish for less problems; wish for more skills.
Don't wish for less challenges; wish for more wisdom."
—*Jim Rohn, speaker, author, philosopher*

As we move into the final chapters of this book, I want to encourage you to develop just one simple "general elevator speech" as part of your day-to-day work/life activity. That way, you will have something polished to say when unplanned, unpredictable circumstances come your way, and you will be poised and ready to really knock it out of the park when a planned opportunity arises. This first elevator speech should be based on just one simple goal or intention, highlighting two or three core arguments or talking points that you can typically count on to generate interest. Start with topics or subjects that seem to interest people the most.

Over time you will draft additional versions on more complex talking points and different subjects, with varying listeners in mind. But for now, at least, start with one general elevator speech in your back pocket so that you will be prepared enough to capitalize on spontaneous elevator speech opportunities whenever they happen!

CRAFTING YOUR FIRST GENERAL ELEVATOR SPEECH

Let's walk through the process of crafting a sample general elevator speech by pulling together all of the ingredients we have discussed throughout the book.

Any effective three-minute elevator speech—whether planned or spontaneous, general or complex, presented in a formal competition or in an office out in the real world—has a unique set of requirements that must be met. For simplicity, I've defined ten basic steps to developing any elevator speech. With those ten steps as a foundation and customized attention to detail, the Elevator Speech Effect can take hold.

NOTE: As I mentioned earlier, there is no single outline that can be used for all situations. It just isn't realistic to have one elevator speech that works with every scenario. After all, we all have different goals and objectives. Nevertheless, with that qualifier in place, we can start with the basics.

Ten Basic Steps to Developing an Elevator Speech

1. **Define your intention.** Ask yourself, "What do I want to happen as a result of my three-minute elevator speech?" Be clear and write out that intention. Remember that your goal is not to score a touchdown in these two to three minutes, just simply and effectively to "advance the ball."

2. **Examine your scenario.** Is this talk for a planned or spontaneous situation? For a planned scenario, it might be helpful to review and use the Presentation Opportunity General Information Form. For an unplanned scenario, your general elevator speech will serve you well. Prepare accordingly, charting the course that will help you earn the right to be heard.

3. **Draft your core outline.** Use the Drafting Your Elevator Speech Outline Worksheet on page 144 to begin. Start by filling in the blanks of the worksheet with a pencil or pen. Start thinking about your messaging, your goals, and your creative ideas, and remember to keep in mind the flow of your talk. What are some of the persuasive arguments you might use in this situation? Structure must be paired with a sense of progression. Your listeners want to know that you're heading somewhere as you build up to your conclusion and close. This is a good time to review Monroe's Motivated Sequence.

4. **Build your case.** Choose your most compelling arguments. Commit to your case points. Explain to your listeners why they need you, your product, or your service; why they need to join your effort; and why now. Avoid using exaggerated superlatives. Provide valid reasons and proof that your arguments pass the "So what?" test.

5. **Don't forget to close.** Think back to your intention. Present your prospect with a clear directive and a respectful call to action. Ask for that next appointment, follow-up call, or meeting. Make it easy and painless for the listener to take the next step with you.

6. **Get creative.** Now that you have your core outline drafted, look it over again through your *creative lens*. It's time to bring your case to life, strategizing your unique and imaginative approach to win over your listener. Dig in and do your homework on your audience or prospects, crafting an approach that speaks directly to their needs. Have some fun and get creative with your openings, illustrations, and closings; grab your listeners' attention and send them home with distinct memories. Avoid being cheesy, but do ramp up your creative nature and customize your talk to dazzle your prospects; give them a reason to want to meet with you again.

7. **Speak in your own voice.** Remember, you are the storyteller. Try a conversational approach that allows you to be comfortable and true to yourself and your personality. Find your voice and communicate your experience, vision, and excitement directly to your prospect in a way that only you can. Reject business boring. Dress up and look your best, polish your vocabulary, move with meaning, and face your fear! You will probably have a more informal, conversational speaking manner in a spontaneous or one-on-one elevator speech opportunity and lean to a slightly more formal speaking manner in a group or planned scenario.

8. **Write it out.** It's helpful to write out your elevator speech in a long version at first, then take a tip from President Ronald Reagan and transfer your core outline and key

points and phrases to an index card. Recite the long version first, and then recite it from the cards to work on your word selection and phrasing. I often tell my clients to "walk through it before you run with it." Eventually, you will not need any notes at all!

9. **Practice. Practice. Practice.** Review your elevator speech again and again until it feels like a natural part of your everyday communication. Remember, it's *your* message. I recommend standing in front of a mirror, resting your notes on the floor, a counter, TV tray, or stand of some sort, and reciting it out loud at least ten times before you test it on your real prospects. It really helps you to see yourself as others see you and to put your focus on sharing the message and not on your notes! Be aware of your presentation length and time the talk with a stopwatch. Also, some people find it helpful to audio-record their presentations and then listen to the playback as if they were the decision maker/listener.

10. **Use it!** Any elevator speech is only effective if you use it, so take it out and let it flow. Morph it, change it, and test it until you find a general speech that you feel comfortable using frequently.

LET'S GO!

Take a few moments to begin crafting your next elevator speech by using the expanded Drafting Your Elevator Speech Outline Worksheet provided. Fill in this worksheet to help you develop your messaging and formulate the progression of your presentation. (Remember, you can also get the free downloads by going to www.smallmessagebigimpact.com.)

DRAFTING YOUR ELEVATOR SPEECH
LONG OUTLINE WORKSHEET

I. INTRODUCTION: **(Attention Step)**

    a. Grab the listener's attention: (Establish a friendly feeling and arouse audience curiosity.)

    ....

    b. Tell the listener where you are going:

    ....

II. BODY

    1. Talking Point #1 *(Ex. Why Me?)*
       a. Argument: **(Need Step)** ....
       b. Proof and/or illustration: **(Satisfaction Step)** ....

       c. So what? What this means to you is . . . **(Visualization Step)**

       ....

    2. Talking Point #2 *(Ex. Why My Organization/Company?)*
       a. Argument: **(Need Step)** ....
       b. Proof and/or illustration: **(Satisfaction Step)** ....

       c. So what? What this means to you is . . . **(Visualization Step)**

       ....

    3. Talking Point #3 *(Ex. Why Now?)*
       a. Argument: **(Need Step)** ....
       b. Proof and/or illustration: **(Satisfaction Step)** ....

       c. So what? What this means to you is . . . **(Visualization Step)**

       ....

III. CONCLUSION: WRAP UP (TRANSITION INTO ACTION STEP)

  ❖ Reiterate the three points (**Conclude the Visualization Step.**)

    ....

  ❖ **Optional:** Suggest a couple of intriguing topics that you can discuss with the listener in your next appointment (Give them a reason to want to hear more.)

    ....

IV. CLOSE: CALL TO ACTION **(Action Step)**

    a. Make your offer of service. State what you want to happen as a result of your elevator speech. (For example: "It is my goal to learn more about your needs and how I might be of service to your company, so that we might work together in some capacity long term.") This serves as a soft transition to your close.

    ....

    ....

    b. Ask for the next appointment time, referral, lead, introduction, next step, opportunity, or whatever will help you initiate the "Elevator Speech Effect."

    ....

A SAMPLE THREE-MINUTE ELEVATOR SPEECH

Let's look at the progressive story of journalist Kari B. She has a twenty-year track record of multiple successes writing and editing for newspapers and magazines. Most people would think this is enough to keep her steadily employed, right? Unfortunately, as the recession has taken its toll on advertising nationwide, print publications are battling to stay afloat. Newspapers and magazines in particular are making deep cuts and scaling back on personnel hours.

Kari wants to supplement her income and have more personal control over her financial situation, so she decides to treat the economic downturn like the opportunity it is and uses this as an entrepreneurial platform from which to generate freelance work. She knows that she can earn money as a freelancer because each day more companies are foregoing full-time employees and hiring contract workers. To fully capitalize on this sea change and sell herself into new opportunities, Kari needs a winning elevator speech that she can present to potential clients—who may or may not know that they need her!

Her first step is to use the Presentation Opportunity General Information Form presented in Chapter 8 on page 126. Kari answers the following simple questions (shown on the next page).

With this information in hand (page 146), Kari drafted the following three-minute elevator speech (pages 147–149) using the Drafting Your Elevator Speech Long Outline Worksheet presented earlier in this chapter.

PRESENTATION OPPORTUNITY
GENERAL INFORMATION

I. WHAT IS THE GOAL OF YOUR PRESENTATION?

To craft a general elevator speech that I can use at a business net-working breakfast in two days. I hope to introduce who I am and how I can be of service, and to set up one-on-one appointment times with potential clients after the breakfast to earn their business as soon as possible and build my client base.

II. AUDIENCE ANALYSIS INFORMATION

- ❖ Who are the listeners? *Small to midsize businesses*
- ❖ Audience size? *Approximately 50 attendees*
- ❖ Average age of group? *30–50*
- ❖ Male-female ratio? *50/50*
- ❖ Attitude of audience? *Busy, come together to network, share ideas*
- ❖ How informed is the audience? *No idea; I am new.*

III. LOGISTICAL INFORMATION

- ❖ Facility *Meeting room at a local hotel*
- ❖ Visual aid options *None. (I guess I could hold up a sample of my work.)*
- ❖ Time allotted for presentation *Three minutes*
- ❖ Who speaks before/after you *Two other new members*

IV. WHAT IS THE BEST WAY TO CLOSE IN THIS SITUATION?

They are in a hurry, and I have to sit down right after I speak, so I will pass out my card and give them a simple handout, "The Top 10 Reasons to Write a White Paper in Today's Market." I will invite them to come see me after the meeting if they would like to set up an appointment time, and I will follow up with them later.

SAMPLE ELEVATOR SPEECH OUTLINE
(LONG VERSION)

I. INTRODUCTION: *(Attention Step)*

    a. Grab the listener's attention:

> *Good morning . . . Imagine yourself in the following scenario. You have been tasked with writing an article for your company newsletter. After hours of frustrating attempts, your computer screen and notepad are still blank. You're not feeling creative. The deadline is approaching. Your writer's block is costing you time and money. What are you going to do? Maybe this scenario isn't so imaginary. If this example is your reality now or possibly in the future, you don't have to go it alone. My name is Kari B. and I might be the solution to your challenge.*

    b. Tell the listener where you are going:

> *You might not know that people like me exist. I am a freelance writer with the ability to pen everything from memos and white papers to marketing materials and feature profiles. During the next few minutes, I'd like to tell you how I can give you peace of mind, save you time, and save you money by using my skills to be your professional writer.*

II. BODY

    1. **Why Me?**

      a. Argument:

> *I can provide you with peace of mind in challenging situations. (Need Step) Have you ever had one of those moments when you knew exactly what you wanted to say but couldn't find the words? (Satisfaction Step) That's where I come in. I have the skills to listen and put your ideas into written form. (Visualization Step) When you partner with me, you will get accurate and authentic messaging as if you had written it yourself.*

b. Proof and/or illustration:

   I am an experienced professional with a degree in journalism. I have specialized in writing and editing.

c. So what?

   What this means to you is, again, peace of mind. No longer will you have to stress out over getting your point across or a looming deadline for a written project. My job is to make you look good.

2. **Why My Organization/Company?**

   a. Argument:

      I can save you time. As I work on a contract basis, you will be able to funnel assignments to me on your schedule and at your convenience, freeing you up to concentrate on other tasks.

   b. Proof and/or illustration:

      How do I do this? I have 18 years of experience in newsrooms where I learned to write fast and accurately. My freelance clients often depend on me to produce materials in as little as 48 to 72 hours.

   c. So what?

      What this means to you is that instead of investing hours in a written project, you can set aside just a few minutes to share your thoughts with me, and then I will have the information I need to proceed, leaving you to move on to other important matters.

3. **Why Now?**

   a. Argument:

      In today's challenging economy, I can save you money by working as an independent contractor.

a. Proof and/or illustration:

My business model is designed to fill in the missing puzzle piece in your company. I offer a competitive rate and have saved many organizations the headache of hiring and training an in-house staff writer.

b. So what?

What this means to you is . . . I can save you the investment of a full-time employee, and give you the opportunity to use that money elsewhere in your business.

I. CONCLUSION: WRAP UP *(Transition Into Action Step)*

So, the next time you are faced with a deadline, or before you get writer's block, I hope you'll pick up the phone and call me first. You don't have to "go it alone." Maybe I can help you with that newsletter article. I can offer you peace of mind, save you time, and maybe even save you some money.

II. CLOSE: CALL TO ACTION *(Action Step)*

❖ What do you want to happen as a result of your elevator speech?

It's my goal to be the writer you choose to work with on your projects.

❖ Ask for the next appointment time, referral, lead, introduction, next step, opportunity, or whatever will help you initiate the "Elevator Speech Effect."

Please come see me after the meeting today and let's set up an appointment to discuss your needs and how I might be of service. When we get together, I will also give you this complimentary tip sheet on the "Top 10 Reasons to Write a White Paper in Today's Market." Thank you for sharing your time with me today.

Use this sample as a guideline whenever you need to deliver a general elevator speech in a group environment. I hope you can also see, however, that this talk could be delivered in a more conversational manner in a one-on-one setting if you focus on the talking points and not necessarily the actual words of the text. I hope sharing Kari B.'s first attempt at a general three-minute elevator speech will inspire you to start thinking about your own presentation.

Now review the short outline sample on page 151. Notice how we condensed the core outline and key points and phrases and transferred them to an index card for use in the field.

Remember, you will still verbally communicate all of the material from your long outline; the short version just serves as a cheat sheet to help you recall your six main components while you're presenting in the field.

151

SAMPLE ELEVATOR SPEECH OUTLINE
SHORT VERSION (4X6 CARD)

I. INTRODUCTION

- Grab the listener's attention: Scenario. Your writer's block is costing you time and money. What are you going to do?
- Tell them where you are going: I am a freelance writer with the ability to pen everything from memos and white papers to marketing materials and feature profiles. Today, I want to briefly share with you how I can . . . .

II. BODY

- Talking Point #1: Why Me? Argument: Give you "peace of mind" in challenging situations. When you partner with me, you will get accurate and authentic messaging as if you had written it yourself.
- Talking Point #2: Why My Organization/Company? Argument: Save you time. As I work on a contract basis, you will be able to funnel assignments to me on your schedule and at your convenience, freeing you up to concentrate on other tasks.
- Talking Point #3: Why Now? Argument: In today's challenging economy, I can save you money by working as an independent contractor.

III. CONCLUSION

- Wrap-up—Reiterate the three points: You don't have to "go it alone." Maybe I can help you with that newsletter article. I can offer you peace of mind, save you time, and maybe even save you some money.

IV. CLOSE: CALL TO ACTION

- Ask for Next Appointment. Offer the complimentary tip sheet on the "Top 10 Reasons to Write a White Paper in Today's Market."

NEXT

It's like a dance. Continually practice and evaluate your elevator speeches in order to improve and grow.

REVIEW
WALK THROUGH IT BEFORE YOU RUN WITH IT

❖ Using our 10-step method, develop one simple "general elevator speech" as part of your day-to-day work/life activity, so that you will be somewhat prepared for those unplanned, unpredictable circumstances.

❖ Use the Presentation Opportunity General Information Form on page 126 to analyze your audience.

❖ Use the (blank) Drafting Your Elevator Speech Worksheet on page 144 to get started.

❖ Use the Blank Elevator Speech Short Outline Form in Chapter 3 on page 44 to condense your talk for street use.

❖ You can use the long and short sample versions as a reference to help you put your next talk together.

eleven

It's a Dance:
Practice and Evaluate
to Improve and Grow

*"A man who carries a cat by the tail learns
something he can learn no other way."*
—Mark Twain

I suspect that even if you have not watched ABC's *Dancing with the Stars*, you have at least heard of this runaway television hit. The wildly popular show, which premiered June 2005, pairs thirteen celebrities with professional dancers for weekly dance competitions. Past seasons have featured athletes, actors, politicians, musicians, and even reality TV stars.

At this point, you might be wondering what *Dancing with the Stars* has in common with crafting a winning three-minute elevator speech. A great deal, actually. Our process of engaging in ongoing goal setting, research, practice, delivery, and evaluation is similar to what unfolds every week on the show.

Let's look closely at how the show's dancers, both professionals and amateurs, prepare for each week's dances. For starters, contestants are given six days to master and perform a choreographed dance routine and perform it for the judges and TV audience. According to the ABC website, "Five hours' practice a day is the secret behind turning two left feet into sweet feet, though the learning process is not without pitfalls."

Each couple is given the same amount of time to prepare and perform. In addition, each couple is given the same basic guidelines about what the judges are expecting. The couples all have the same goal: to advance to the next round, avoid elimination, and win! And yet, no dance is ever performed in exactly the same way by the competing couples. Each performance reflects the preparation, natural talent, personality, and determination of the dancers themselves.

PULLING IT ALL TOGETHER

The average dance routine on the show is a little longer than a minute, and yet, each week a huge amount of physical exercise, choreography, and practice are required of the dancers to pull their performance together. At showtime, everything matters, including the costumes, elaborate hairstyles, stage makeup, props, music, lighting, and the all-important timing. Quite a few puzzle pieces must come together—just like in any great presentation—to nail the performance and declare it a success.

As usual, the beautiful, graceful dancers make it look so easy and fun at the moment of execution, but each week the show offers a sneak peek at the rehearsals for every dance. Those rehearsals make it clear that "to dance with the stars" isn't just a lot of glitz and fun and that the dancers never just wing it!

> "Experience is the teacher of all things."
> —Julius Caesar

After days of grueling workouts and practices, they take their performance to the dance floor where the judges—Carrie Ann Inaba, Len Goodman, and Bruno Tonioli—comment on and evaluate everything from technical execution to style and creativity. Did the couple bring the dance to life? Did they convey the passion of the mambo or the flirtatiousness of the cha-cha or the elegance of the waltz? The judges' answers are interesting, and sometimes colorful, as they offer insight on how the dancers can improve, tweak, and enhance their performances in the next round—should they survive. On any given week, you'll hear comments like these:

> "Tricks aren't necessary . . . When you kept it classic, it worked."
>
> "Simplicity is often the best route to success."
>
> "You really 'pushed it' this week . . . This was a very difficult routine, and you made a couple of mistakes, but you pulled it off! Congratulations!"
>
> "You seemed a little off balance."
>
> "You need to work on your lines and curves."
>
> "You made a mistake, but you kept on going, and you finished the routine and that is the most important part."

The participants, in turn, are interviewed by one of the co-hosts backstage after receiving their scores for each dance. The comments of the performers themselves are as interesting as the feedback from the judges; their comments will also sound familiar to anyone who is training and attempting to engage in a new skill or activity:

"I knew going into this week that we've really gotta focus. We've really gotta step it up!"

"My partner is amazing. I want to show the judges that I can get better every week!"

"During the training and practice, we worked really hard. I had to learn new moves. We took some risks. It was hard, but it was fun. I am learning a lot and having a great time."

"It feels so different from what I am used to."

"It was really uncomfortable at first!"

"I would get soooo frustrated!"

"This week I was so busy with other things and really short on time to practice the routine, and it may have shown in my performance."

"I was very driven in rehearsal . . . and I am proud of my effort, but it's not perfect. Yet!"

"I was concentrating so much, it just came off a little stiff . . . I need to work on the flow!"

"I am really happy with our performance tonight . . . Let's do it again, and again and again!"

"I keep improving and that's what matters!"

Interestingly, these reflections and statements are very similar to those comments shared by participants in our workshops.

In the end, it's not all about winning, and there's not a big money prize. At the finale, the competitors talk about how the experience has changed them, pushed them out of their comfort zone, and forced them to try new things and to view life from a different perspective. They usually agree that the experience has enriched other areas of their lives.

For many of the celebrities, it's a new technique and skill set they can apply to their work, and it enhances what they are already good at. Nice!

EVALUATE YOUR PERFORMANCE

Now that you have crafted a general elevator speech, it's time to get out on the dance floor if you will. Take a final look at your presentation and remember to use solid, relevant arguments, creative examples, and your own, unique voice to reach your audience. For this practice run, you will need two things:

1. **Stopwatch**—You will want to accurately measure how long it takes to deliver your talk. Some competitions will give you two minutes; others will give you three minutes. In the real world, some people might give you three minutes, as Donald Trump did with Ricardo Bellino in the story you read in Chapter 2. By using a stopwatch you'll develop a sense of time and thus be able to honor the time limits, both real and implied, when you deliver your talk.

2. **Speech Evaluation Form**—On page 161 you will find the Speech Evaluation Form that we use in our Sjodin Communications workshops. (You can also get the free

downloads by going to www.smallmessagebigimpact.com. Print this form on letter-size paper for ease of use.)

TAKE IT TO THE STREETS

With these tools in hand, you are ready for a serious practice run or your first real-world presentation. After you present, don't forget to complete a self-evaluation. Evaluation, while sometimes uncomfortable and disheartening, is essential to recognizing your missteps and learning how to correct them. Here are a few scenarios:

Work on your own. As suggested in Chapter 10, try watching yourself in a mirror when practicing on your own. Use an audio-recorder so you can listen to the playback and hear your talk as if you were the listener. Then complete the evaluation form on your own and don't be too hard on yourself.

Enlist a friend. Ask a friend or mentor to evaluate your elevator speech using a blank copy of the Speech Evaluation Form. Be sure they have at least read this book ahead of time so they understand the principles, goals, and benchmarks you are striving for before they evaluate your performance.

Develop a small group evaluation session. Bring together a small group of committed associates and create a space where everyone will participate in a positive and supportive environment. Take turns delivering your talks and sharing completed evaluation forms and feedback.

Schedule a formal practice workshop within your organization. Invite colleagues to show up and practice their speeches in front of each other for helpful feedback.

Self-evaluate after giving a live real-world talk. Upon returning home from an actual presentation, take time to evaluate your message, noting what you did well and what needs improvement.

In each of these scenarios, whether you are by yourself or in a group, completing the Speech Evaluation Form is helpful. You will be able to see how your talk played to a real audience. You will be able to see yourself in real time and understand where you might be running into trouble. Self-evaluation is the key to morphing your talk for future effectiveness, and it can help you assess whether or not the Elevator Speech Effect was successfully set into motion.

LET'S REVIEW THE SPEECH EVALUATION FORM

The Speech Evaluation Form is divided into three main sections: building, creativity, and delivery. Each section asks questions to make sure the speaker is on track and meeting each benchmark.

SPEECH EVALUATION FORM

PRESENTERS NAME:

BUILDING A PERSUASIVE CASE	Needs Work	Fine	Excellent	CREATIVITY	Needs Work	Fine	Excellent	AUTHENTIC DELIVERY	Needs Work	Fine	Excellent
Did the speaker:											
1. Use a structured outline?				1. Grab the listener's attention?				1. Have energy and enthusiasm and/or engage the audience's attention with their presence?			
a. Introduction				2. Make the message interesting or thought provoking?				2. Have good diction, word choice, and use of vocabulary?			
b. Body				3. Use engaging anecdotes, stories, and other support to create a compelling message?				3. Avoid distracting body language and engage in effective use of movement?			
c. Conclusion				4. Present an interesting analysis to the audience?				4. Use effective volume, rate, pacing, and range in the way they speak and present?			
d. Close				5. Tell stories that relate to the audience?				5. Display confidence and speak in their own authentic voice?			
2. Make the intention clear?				6. Cite sources to provide convincing evidence to support claims?				6. Use visual aids effectively?			
3. Craft clean, logical arguments to support their case?								7. Dress appropriately?			
4. Address the needs of the audience?											
5. Use the allotted time in a balanced, effective manner?											
6. Have a clear call to action?											
7. Use the bridge line, "What this means to you is . . ."?											
Notes:											

EVALUATOR: _____   TIME: _____

Building

Did the speaker:

- ❖ Use a structured outline?
  - Introduction
  - Body
  - Conclusion
  - Close
- ❖ Make the intention clear?
- ❖ Craft clean, logical arguments to support his/her case?
- ❖ Address the needs of the audience?
- ❖ Use the allotted time in a balanced, effective manner?
- ❖ Have a clear call to action?
- ❖ Use the bridge line, "What this means to you is . . ."?

NOTE: What we are looking for here is the speaker's ability to craft the foundation of his/her case.

Creativity

Did the speaker:

- ❖ Grab the listener's attention?
- ❖ Make the message interesting or thought provoking?
- ❖ Use engaging anecdotes, stories, and other support to create a compelling message?
- ❖ Present an interesting analysis to the audience?

❖ Tell stories that relate to the audience?

❖ Cite sources to provide convincing evidence to support claims?

NOTE: What we are looking for here is the speaker's ability to bring the case to life by using stories, anecdotes, creative analysis, and thought-provoking messaging.

Delivery

Did the speaker:

❖ Have energy and enthusiasm and/or engage the audience's attention with his/her presence?

❖ Have good diction, word choice, and use of vocabulary?

❖ Avoid distracting body language and engage in effective use of movement?

❖ Use effective volume, rate, pacing, and range in the way he/she spoke?

❖ Display confidence and speak in his/her authentic voice?

❖ Use visual aids effectively?

❖ Dress appropriately?

NOTE: What we are looking for here is the speaker's ability to bring his/her elevator speech together, using delivery skills to combine all of the pieces of the puzzle and to complete the picture.

 You can print out a letter-size copy of the Speech Evaluation Form from the "Free Downloads" section at www. smallmessagebigimpact.com.

IT'S GOOD TO BE GREEN

Remember, this is a learning process. Be kind to yourself and to others. As I mentioned earlier, "When you're green you're growing, and when you're ripe you're rotting." It's good to be green. You want to keep in mind that practice and evaluation are all just part of the process of improving and growing. Just like on *Dancing with the Stars*, the moves might seem awkward in the beginning, but the more you practice, the quicker you will eventually reach the point where you are performing a beautiful, flowing dance.

NEXT

As you begin to deliver your elevator speech in the real world, there might be hurdles and challenges that will present themselves. In the next chapter, we will answer some of your most frequently asked questions.

REVIEW
IT'S A DANCE: PRACTICE AND EVALUATE
TO IMPROVE AND GROW

❖ Our process of engaging in goal setting, research, practice, delivery, and evaluation is similar to what unfolds every week on *Dancing with the Stars*.

❖ In the end, it's not all about winning; it's also about enjoying the journey and exploring the dance. I hope you will find that the experience has changed you, pushed you out of your comfort zone, and forced you to try new things and to view life from a different perspective.

❖ Practice and watch your time. Use a stopwatch to accurately measure how long it takes to deliver your talk. It is important to be aware of and honor the time limits, both real and implied, in delivering your talk.

❖ Enlist a friend or mentor to evaluate your elevator speech using a blank copy of the Speech Evaluation Form. Be sure they understand the principles, goals, and benchmarks you are striving for before they evaluate your performance.

❖ Host an evaluation session for a small group of committed associates and create a space where everyone will participate in a positive and supportive environment. Take turns delivering your talks and sharing completed evaluation forms and feedback.

❖ Upon returning home from an actual presentation, take time to evaluate your elevator speech, noting what you did well and what needs improvement.

twelve

Nuggets of Advice and Answers to Frequently Asked Questions

We all face challenges as we go through our day-to-day activities: preparing for meetings, giving presentations, and handling other opportunities that arise. In taking the steps necessary to move our lives and professions forward, we sometimes have questions or hit obstacles that are seemingly difficult to overcome. That's when we want and need guidance. I often find myself wishing I had a coach or mentor whispering sound advice in my ear at just the right moment. Sometimes I reflect on a presentation that didn't go as well as I had hoped and wish I had asked for more insight or advice before proceeding.

There have been other times when a mentor or colleague gave me advice and I didn't want to hear it, or I even ignored it when I should have listened. Many times I have declared myself "just too busy" to stop and make the effort to listen, read, and see things from the perspectives of guides along the way. Has this ever happened to you?

This is so beautifully illustrated in the movie *The Legend of Bagger Vance*, a 2000 DreamWorks release directed by Robert Redford, starring Matt Damon, Will Smith, and Charlize Theron. Damon played Rannulph Junuh, a disillusioned young man who returned from the battlefields of war with a broken spirit and turned his back on the world, that is, until the day he is asked to participate in a golf tournament. He unwillingly accepts, and then a mysterious stranger, Bagger Vance, portrayed by Smith, enters the picture and helps Junuh "find his swing." Bagger is a subtle and colorful spiritual guide and golf caddy who miraculously steps in and helps Junuh turn his life around.

Junuh is, at times, negative, positive, hopeful, depressed, confrontational, angry, cocky, and defiant—certainly not the perfect student. Though his pupil is reluctant to listen and learn from him, Bagger shares with Junuh pearls of wisdom that make a significant and positive difference in Junuh's journey.

I encourage you to rent this movie, and therefore I don't want to spoil the ending for you. Suffice it to say that in the end, with the inspiration and guidance from Bagger, Junuh is able to grow through his challenges and come out the other side victorious—personally, spiritually, and professionally.

Clearly, I'm no Bagger Vance, but when it comes to three-minute elevator speeches, I want to help you see the field from a different focus and help you understand you have a lot of different shots to choose from. Ideally, I hope you are beginning to notice the nuances on the playing field and will start having more fun doing what it is that you do every day. And, although I can't take you there, I hope I can help you find a new perspective.

FREQUENTLY ASKED QUESTIONS

While I cannot be with you out on the course, if you will, I can respond to the common objections, hurdles, and challenges that present themselves once you are engaged in practicing and delivering your elevator speeches.

The questions and comments you are about to read are real. The names of individuals have been omitted because I respect their privacy, but I am confident you can benefit from the answers and share in the learning nonetheless. Some of these FAQs are concerns and comments I hear in the field, including simple mistakes that are easy to correct, but if they are left uncorrected, they can undermine an elevator speech, stand in the way of the magic of the Elevator Speech Effect, and create roadblocks on the path to achieving your goals. I hope the answers help you "find your swing."

Q: I have this little voice in my head that is screaming: "I have been in this business a very long time. I can just walk into a situation and wing it. Why do I need an elevator speech?"

A: I have great respect for those who have worked in their profession for years. There is significance and credibility that comes with having extensive background and experience in any industry. That said, I just cannot imagine anyone undervaluing the importance of continued growth, and preparation for different situations at all levels of experience. When I heard this question, it made me think of people who have reached the top of their fields through sheer discipline and practice. People like guitarist Eric Clapton, women's soccer pioneer Michelle Akers, cyclist

Lance Armstrong, Academy Award-winning actress Meryl Streep, NFL receiver Jerry Rice and world-class tennis champions Venus and Serena Williams. I also thought of Tiger Woods, (let's set his personal challenges to the side) who is on track to be the winningest golfer in history. He has been in the business of professional golf (and quite successfully) for a long time, and yet he still walks the course before every tournament and is said to put in more practice and prep time than almost any other golfer on the circuit today. Clearly, with all of his tenure, experience, and winning track record, Tiger could wing it. At this point in their careers, all of these professionals could wing it. But they don't. I trust that it is their commitment to continued practice, evolution of their skills and preparation that keep them consistent champions.

Q: Everyone goes after the "Big Fish." How can I possibly beat out the seasoned pros to get in the door and land the major clients?

A: You do it one at a time. Begin by making a list of your dream clients and doing your homework on each one individually, finding the best approach for each person. Sometimes you have to really get creative to find a way in.

A humorous example of extreme creativity in going after the Big Fish is in the classic 1988 movie *Working Girl*, a romantic comedy starring Melanie Griffith, Sigourney Weaver, and Harrison Ford.

Melanie Griffith plays Tess, a thirty-year-old, hardworking gal who went to school at night after working 9 to 5 in the secretarial pool during the day. She is trying to pay her dues and work her way up the ladder in the business world of mergers and acquisitions, but she just can't get a break. Then, when Tess discovers that the power hungry woman she works for is trying to steal her idea and claim it as her own, she decides to take matters into her own hands.

When her conniving boss takes a spill off a mountain while skiing and is out of the office for a few weeks, Tess seizes the opportunity and decides to pitch her idea to the client on her own. But how will she do it? First, she needs Jack, a man who has the connections to make a deal. In order to get Jack on board, she pretends to be someone she is not (her boss's counterpart, not her secretary). Prepared with data, she pitches an idea for the potential deal and he takes the bait. Now, together they must approach a certain CEO, Mr. Trask. But time is running out. How will she get to him?

In an example of sublimely scrappy behavior, Tess persuades Jack to accompany her to the wedding of Trask's daughter. Looking like they belong in the posh hotel where the lavish reception is being held, Tess and Jack not only crash the party but Tess also maneuvers her way over to Trask and dances with him. And that is when she delivers her elevator speech.

She knows that the gentleman is distracted—it is his daughter's wedding, after all—but he still gives her the courtesy of listening to her brief pitch. He is an aggressive businessman, too. Tess's goal is to close for the next appointment time, and her gutsy strategy pays off. She gets the meeting.

Now, I am not suggesting that you crash weddings to present ideas. As a matter of fact, to avoid any confusion, I must say, "Please don't!" It's just a movie. Still, I found a little inspiration in the story. Look at the progression that Tess took. Frustrated and hemmed in at her job, she wanted to succeed, and so she prepared, always doing her homework. Then, in a giant leap of faith in herself, she moved across a room to speak to the person who could change her circumstances. And that is exactly what happened—including ending up with Jack.

OK, this was a romantic comedy, and everything usually works out in the heroine's best interest in these movies. That said, I hope it serves to inspire you to find your own unique approach to capture the attention of a Big Fish.

> **Q: I think it is important to have a lot of information in my elevator speech, but you say we need to be more persuasive. If we give them enough good information, won't our listeners be more willing to buy?**
>
> A: Yes and no. Yes, it is important to have quality information to support the points in your case. But, no, not a lot, and if you end up doing an information dump and you don't craft intriguing points in the body of your message, your elevator speech could end up sounding far too informative versus persuasive, and it will be a challenge to intrigue the listener enough to get them to want to book the next appointment time with you.

NOTE: The two most common critiques that I hear from people after they've watched their own presentations and completed their own self-evaluations are: "I felt maybe I went a little too long, and I think it got a little boring." So I ask them, "If you thought it was getting long and you thought it was getting boring, why did you keep going?" And they usually say, "Well, gosh, Terri, I have to get out all the information!" My response to that is, "What is the point of doing a data dump if you are perceived as being long and boring?"

The best presentations are a combination of rock-solid case points and quality information that supports the arguments, with clever ideas and illustrations that bring it to life. Beware of two common pitfalls: being far more informative than persuasive, and being boring.

Q: I got my three minutes and the time flew by. I didn't hit all the points I wanted to make. How do I manage the time?

A: You have to practice out loud and get a feel for managing your time. A good general first step is to divide your speech into balanced yet appropriate lengths: approximately thirty seconds per component for the introduction, for each of the three persuasive points, for the conclusion, and for the close. As you practice, you will develop almost a sixth sense about the timing. After a while, you will better understand how to flow through your content with smooth transitions from talking point to talking point. The best way to stay on track is to literally track the time and become aware of what it feels like when the clock is ticking.

Q: I started my elevator speech and the audience seemed bored after thirty seconds! Now what?

A: Recording and reviewing yourself is helpful. Imagine that you are the listener and ask yourself, "Would this grab my attention?" Make sure you have an interesting approach, a compelling analysis, and/or clever, creative arguments. It almost sounds cliché, but you want to awaken the curiosity of your listeners.

Q: You use three minutes as your base time allotment for an elevator speech. What if they only give me one minute?

A: Take it! In this case, you will most likely have to reduce your content outline to only one main point, but still follow the basic structure: an introduction, one body point, a conclusion, and a close. It can be challenging, but don't walk away from this opportunity, even if it's only a minute.

Q: Can I use props in my elevator speech?

A: Yes, but not too many. It is appropriate to hold up examples of products and services, but do not go overboard. A visual aid should be a tool that enhances your talk. It should be used to say something visually that you cannot communicate in the same way verbally. Do not let your visual aids upstage you or you could lose control of the situation.

Q: I get so nervous. How can I manage my nervous energy?

A: Understand that everyone gets nervous. It is natural. On the most basic level, if you are not a little nervous, it means that you probably are not pushing yourself too far outside of your comfort zone. If you are nervous, keep it to yourself and remember it is OK! (It makes you feel alive!) There is little to be gained by sharing it with your audience because they might perceive you as unprepared or as less competent than you actually are. On those days when I have pushed myself and felt a little nervous, I could always lay my head on the pillow that night and think, "Good day!"

Q: I have heard it's better to "dress down" and have a more casual appearance to meet with prospects in today's market. Is that true?

A: I feel this is urban legend dressed up as fact. I have not personally read any research that suggests dressing down for a professional presentation has ever worked for the presenter. In my opinion, you should dress up to show your respect for your listener's or prospect's time and that you honor the privilege of speaking to him/her. When you are dressed up, clean, fresh, and pressed, you carry yourself differently. You send a message of confidence and professionalism. Here's an example.

A friend was interviewing for a position with an Internet marketing company, and within minutes of walking through the door to meet with the company's founder and CEO, he was complimented on the fact that he was wearing a suit. The CEO actually commented to my friend that he was blown away by how many people come in for an interview in jeans or just dress pants and nice shirts, which immediately disinterests him in them as candidates for the position. The CEO said people think that casual dress rules in the technology industry. That's simply not the case in today's market, and certainly not when you are meeting with someone for the first time.

The late, legendary syndicated commentator and radio news talk show host Paul Harvey always wore a suit and tie with all of the appropriate accessories when doing his radio show. In an interview on March 1, 2009, with Larry King, King asked Harvey why he was always so dressed up for his radio show when obviously no one could see him, and he responded: "I can't explain why. But I do know that the times I've tried to go casual... something is sacrificed." Larry said, "You're not as good?" And Paul responded, "I don't know if good is the word. I can't put my finger on it. But I do know something is missing." (A transcript of the interview is available at http://transcripts.cnn.com/TRANSCRIPTS/0903/01/lkl.01.html.)

Q: I gave my elevator speech, but nothing happened. What can I say at the end of my presentations to get the next appointment time?

A: What do you want to happen as a result of your elevator speech? Your intention will point you in the right direction toward your closing line or phrase. Remember to stay conversational. Keep it simple and don't oversell. What you will say depends on what you want to have happen. Try something like, "How would I go about setting up the next appointment time with you?" It's not a yes or no question, and it gently pushes the listener in the direction you want to go. Bottom line? Even if you are a bit uncomfortable, you have to gracefully ask for that next appointment.

Q: What if they say, "No thanks"?

A: That's okay. Thank them for their time and walk away like a lady or a gentleman. It's not the end of the world. Reassess your messaging and your delivery, shake it off, and try again. No drama. Maybe next time or maybe the next listener. Just enjoy the ride.

Q: Why do we need an elevator speech? We have been working with this company for a long time, and we are number one in our industry, so we always get meetings with clients.

A: So what? Do not get lazy. With all of the constant changes in today's markets, you have to continually earn the right to be heard by new people. It is great to have solid contacts, but you should develop a plan for the succession of people. If your key contacts go away, you want to have other people in place who can support, recommend, and endorse you.

Q: My company provides a very sophisticated, complex product. It is impossible to sell the "whole enchilada" in three minutes.

A: You are not supposed to. You have to look at the three-minute elevator speech as part of an overall process. Remember that the intention of the elevator speech is not to score the touchdown but to advance the ball. The purpose of those three minutes is to intrigue your audience with a glimpse of that sophisticated, complex product and secure another appointment in the future.

Q: I just listened to the playback of my three-minute elevator speech, and I sound so "business boring." What do I do?

A: You might have focused too heavily on the case portion of your speech and not enough on the creativity and delivery. Ask yourself how you can inject more creativity, more of your natural personality, voice, and style, into your talk, which can help you find greater harmony within your message.

Q: I am so nervous. What if I mess up?

A: So what? I know that might sound crazy or flip, but I would rather you try and mess up than never try at all. Odds are, your first elevator speech won't be great. But in time, your talks will get better, your successes will increase, and the opportunities will increase. We all have that fear of failure, but you just have to go for it. Like the old proverb says, "If at first you don't succeed, try, try again." Each time you set a higher goal, or set a new standard for yourself, you will have to enhance or build on your skill set. First a novice, then an intermediate, then an advanced, and then a pro. From there, the sky's the limit.

Q: I did it once and it worked. Can I do the same thing again with another contact?

A: Absolutely. Why reinvent the wheel? When an Olympic gymnast scores a perfect 10 on a floor routine, she keeps performing it over and over. Take what works for you and use it with other listeners, prospects, and clients.

Q: I'm just not creative. I can't think of anything clever. Will you write my elevator speech?

A: I could, but I'm trying to help you be independent of me, not dependent on me. Just follow the outline and you will get the hang of it. Watch others and learn with them and from them. Practice, get coaching, execute!

Q: When I am at a trade show I have to give my pitch so many times my voice is tired. Any suggestions?

A: Yes, that's normal. I usually stay away from caffeinated drinks or beverages with creamers. My standard remedy is sipping on hot water mixed with honey and lemon. It always soothes my throat. If it get's really bad maybe you should take shorter shifts in the booth or see a doctor for a professional diagnosis.

Q: I told a joke and it bombed. I saw another guy in my office use it and it was great. I am just not funny. What can I do?

A: Do not assume that you can re-create another person's humor. The safest approach is to choose material that is appropriate for you and your personality. Speak in your own voice and from your own experiences and you will feel more at ease.

NOTE: Don't feel bad. Sometimes finding out what works for you begins by figuring out what does not work.

Q: Can you use a handout for an elevator speech?

A: Yes, you can actually use it in a couple of places: before you get started, if you have that luxury, or at the end, as a leave-behind for audience members.

Q: Can I use notes?

A: Yes and no. Clearly, President Ronald Reagan used notes, as I discussed in Chapter 9. When speaking at a podium in a more formal group setting, notes are appropriate and helpful. But if you're standing on a golf course or in a buffet line or in a hallway, you will not have the luxury of notes. It's best to learn to present your speech or talking points without notes.

Q: Can I use a gimmick to get my listeners to ask me for my card at the end of my elevator speech?

A: Yes, especially in a group environment. The business card trade is a great way to step into the next appointment opportunity. I am not sure about the word "gimmick." I am assuming you mean that at the end of your speech you might tell your audience that you will trade a certain object (free pens, tip sheets, gift cards, writing pads, etc.) for a business card. That might work; just be careful not to let things get too circus-like. Your goal is to enhance your credibility, not undermine it. So, proceed with caution, unless you are really going to "put it into high gear and ham it up" with humor.

Q: Does my elevator speech have to be three minutes?

A: No. You can morph and twist and tweak your speech as you see fit. We have found that, universally, three minutes is a reasonable amount of time to grab someone's attention and ask them for an appointment. Some prefer two minutes. When you have the chance or option, go for three.

Q: I tend to get very excited and talk really fast. Maybe I am trying to squeeze too much into my elevator speech. What can I do?

A: That's a good assessment. Remember to relax and speak in a calm, conversational voice. You want your information to flow. Just a nice, easy walk in the park.

Q: I want to create a need for my service, but I don't want to sound too negative or like a fearmonger. I don't want to send a message of doom and gloom!

A: There is a balance between creating a need and providing a solution, on the one hand, and generating fear. You might use one example of a really heavy subject but no more. You can forgo the fear and negativity and still create a sense of urgency and need for your product or service.

Q: How many times do I need to practice this thing?

A: Until you feel like you "own it." Remember, polish comes from practice, but charisma comes from certainty. In general, I recommend practicing your elevator speech at least 10 times in its entirety before you take it out into the field.

Q: What is the hardest product or service to sell?

A: The one you don't believe in.

conclusion

A Personal Letter from Terri

To the Readers,

As I conclude this book, I would like to share a few personal thoughts and feelings with you. First of all, nobody's perfect. I have seen amazing presenters when they are really "on" and I have seen them when they are "off." We all have good days and bad days, and that's OK. I am not the perfect speechwriter or the perfect speech coach or the perfect sales presenter. Far from perfect. The good news is that it really doesn't have to be perfect to work! All we can do is give it our best effort, practice, and try to consistently have more on days than off days.

I do love the art, form, and science of speech communication. I am now and will continue to be a student of this practice because I feel it makes me a better presenter, coach, and consultant. I have mellowed over the years. I am still scrappy but not as aggressive as I was when I was younger. Time and experience change us all. They make us wiser and teach us to listen with a different perspective. I laugh at myself, at some of the things I have done, at approaches that I have tried. But through the trial and error, I have found my voice and my ever-changing self.

I am grateful for my past and I look forward to viewing the future through a different lens. I have found that by learning with and from friends, colleagues, mentors, students, and peers who participate in developing more polished and persuasive messaging, we have all grown and had more consistent, positive outcomes that have led to amazing opportunities. I have written elevator speeches that have worked really well and those that haven't. Some worked for awhile then not again. I have coached people who got the deal they wanted on the first try and some who didn't get it until several attempts later. I have won and lost in competitions and in business and that's all OK. I am enjoying the ride.

It has been my intention in writing this book to make the road a bit easier, a bit faster, a little more fun, and a lot more successful for you on your journey. I hope I have. So, there you have it. My best effort (for now) on the Elevator Speech Effect. I reserve the right to change, morph, and grow this material in the future. Trust in yourself and your ability. You can do this. Give yourself a chance. Give your dream a chance. Go forth with hope. Small messages have a big impact! Ask yourself, "Why not me?" Why not you!

Sincerely,
Terri L. Sjodin

appendix

What follows is a blank copy of each of the forms listed below:

- ❖ Blank Elevator Speech Short Outline Form (Chapter 3)
- ❖ Six Point Star Method Diagram (Chapter 7)
- ❖ Presentation Opportunity General Information Form (Chapter 8)
- ❖ Drafting Your Elevator Speech Long Outline Worksheet (Chapter 10)
- ❖ Speech Evaluation Form (Chapter 11)

Special nugget for our readers! In addition to the blank forms in this appendix, you can access a larger version of each document by going to www.smallmessagebigimpact.com.

From the home page, click on the stopwatch/butterfly icon in the upper right-hand corner. This will take you to the "Small Message, Big Impact® Free Downloads" page. To receive the access code for the "Small Message, Big Impact® Free Downloads," please enter your email address in the simple registration form. This will automatically add you to a subscribers' list to receive the complimentary *Presenters Post* quarterly e-newsletter, and you will be sent the special access code for the "Small Message, Big Impact® Free Downloads" page via return email.

BLANK ELEVATOR SPEECH SHORT OUTLINE FORM (4X6 CARD)

I. INTRODUCTION
- Grab the listener's attention
- Tell them where you are going

II. BODY
- Talking point #1
- Talking point #2
- Talking point #3

III. CONCLUSION
- Wrap up. (Allude to a couple of strong points you wish to discuss in detail if given additional time.)

IV. CLOSE: CALL TO ACTION
- Ask for an appointment time to give them a longer, more in-depth presentation.

Available for download at www.smallmessagebigimpact.com

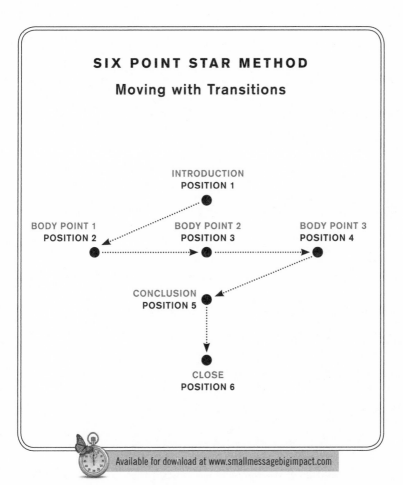

SIX POINT STAR METHOD

Moving with Transitions

INTRODUCTION
POSITION 1

BODY POINT 1   BODY POINT 2   BODY POINT 3
POSITION 2   **POSITION 3**   **POSITION 4**

CONCLUSION
POSITION 5

CLOSE
POSITION 6

Available for download at www.smallmessagebigimpact.com

PRESENTATION OPPORTUNITY
GENERAL INFORMATION FORM

I. WHAT IS THE GOAL OF YOUR PRESENTATION?

....

....

II. WHAT IS YOUR INTENTION?

....

....

III. AUDIENCE ANALYSIS INFORMATION

❖ Who are the listeners? ....

❖ Audience size? ....

❖ Average age of group? ....

❖ Male-female ratio? ....

❖ Attitude of audience? ....

❖ How informed is the audience? ....

IV. LOGISTICAL INFORMATION

❖ Facility ....

❖ Visual aid options ....

❖ Time alloted for presentation ....

❖ Who speaks before/after you ....

V. WHAT IS THE BEST WAY TO CLOSE IN THIS SITUATION?

....

....

DRAFTING YOUR ELEVATOR SPEECH
LONG OUTLINE WORKSHEET

I. INTRODUCTION: **(Attention Step)**

    a. Grab the listener's attention: (Establish a friendly feeling and arouse audience curiosity.)

    ....

    b. Tell the listener where you are going:

    ....

II. BODY

    1. Talking Point #1 *(Ex. Why Me?)*
       a. Argument: **(Need Step)** ....
       b. Proof and/or illustration: **(Satisfaction Step)** ....

       c. So what? What this means to you is . . . **(Visualization Step)**

    ....

    2. Talking Point #2 *(Ex. Why My Organization/Company?)*
       a. Argument: **(Need Step)** ....
       b. Proof and/or illustration: **(Satisfaction Step)** ....

       c. So what? What this means to you is . . . **(Visualization Step)**

    ....

    3. Talking Point #3 *(Ex. Why Now?)*
       a. Argument: **(Need Step)** ....
       b. Proof and/or illustration: **(Satisfaction Step)** ....

       c. So what? What this means to you is . . . **(Visualization Step)**

    ....

III. CONCLUSION: WRAP UP (TRANSITION INTO ACTION STEP)

    ❖ Reiterate the three points **(Conclude the Visualization Step.)**

    ....

    ❖ **Optional:** Suggest a couple of intriguing topics that you can discuss with the listener in your next appointment (Give them a reason to want to hear more.)

    ....

IV. CLOSE: CALL TO ACTION **(Action Step)**

    a. Make your offer of service. State what you want to happen as a result of your elevator speech. (For example: "It is my goal to learn more about your needs and how I might be of service to your company, so that we might work together in some capacity long term.") This serves as a soft transition to your close.

    ....
    ....

    b. Ask for the next appointment time, referral, lead, introduction, next step, opportunity, or whatever will help you initiate the "Elevator Speech Effect."

    ....

SPEECH EVALUATION FORM

PRESENTER'S NAME: _____

BUILDING A PERSUASIVE CASE

	Needs Work	Fine	Excellent
Did the speaker:			
1. Use a structured outline?			
a. Introduction			
b. Body			
c. Conclusion			
d. Close			
2. Make the intention clear?			
3. Craft clean, logical arguments to support their case?			
4. Address the needs of the audience?			
5. Use the allotted time in a balanced, effective manner?			
6. Have a clear call to action?			
7. Use the bridge line, "What this means to you is . . ."?			

Notes:

CREATIVITY

	Needs Work	Fine	Excellent
1. Grab the listener's attention?			
2. Make the message interesting or thought provoking?			
3. Use engaging anecdotes, stories, and other support to create a compelling message?			
4. Present an interesting analysis to the audience?			
5. Tell stories that relate to the audience?			
6. Cite sources to provide convincing evidence to support claims?			

AUTHENTIC DELIVERY

	Needs Work	Fine	Excellent
1. Have energy and enthusiasm and/or engage the audience's attention with their presence?			
2. Have good diction, word choice, and use of vocabulary?			
3. Avoid distracting body language and engage in effective use of movement?			
4. Use effective volume, rate, pacing, and range in the way they speak and present?			
5. Display confidence and speak in their own authentic voice?			
6. Use visual aids effectively?			
7. Dress appropriately?			

EVALUATOR: _____   TIME: _____

index

Websites and Related Sources

Wake Forest Elevator Speech Competition: Babock Graduate School of Management, Wake Forest University, Winston-Salem, N.C. www.business.wfu.edu/default.aspx?id=268

Make Mine a Million $ Business: Sponsored by Count Me In, www.makemineamillion.org

Tech Coast Angels: www.techcoastangels.com

Dr. Wayne Dyer: www.drwaynedyer.com

Selling Power: www.sellingpower.com

Success: www.successmagazine.com

National Speakers Association: www.nsaspeaker.org

more info...

Small Message, Big Impact®: How to Put the Power of the Elevator Speech Effect to Work for You!

Audio program, read by the author
Total Playing Time: Approximately 4 ½ hours
Set includes 5 Audio CD Disks and 1 Data Disk

Small Message, Big Impact® Workbook & Study Guide

A practical companion to *Small Message, Big Impact®*, this workbook will help you transform inspired thoughts into tangible results. Exercise by exercise, you will follow a roadmap to craft an elevator speech for your message. Each session was created to spark your creativity, generate ideas, and spur you to action. The questions and activities were chosen with both individuals and groups in mind and can be applied across a full spectrum of professions and endeavors. Use this workbook after you read *Small Message, Big Impact®* as part of a book club, study group or spaced learning program and put the *Elevator Speech Effect* to work for you!

New Sales Speak: The 9 Biggest Sales Presentation Mistakes and How to Avoid Them, 2nd Edition
Published by John Wiley & Sons
978-0471755654

This book identifies the most common mistakes individuals make when presenting and explains how to avoid them when creating your own highly successful presentation. Including a detailed sample outline you can adapt for your own purposes. This book will turn you into a polished and persuasive professional and a first-class presenter.

Mentoring: The Most Obvious Yet Overlooked Key to Achieving More in Life than You Dreamed Possible
Published by McGraw-Hill
978-0786311354

Mentoring reveals the secrets to achieving high degrees of success: personal, professional, economic, and emotional through a series of stories and letters illustrating mentoring relationships.

As this book explains, anyone can maximize their potential with the help of the right mentor. Readers will discover how to create a successful mentoring lifestyle, including: four basic reasons why mentoring works.

For more information regarding Terri Sjodin's programs and materials please visit:
www.sjodincommunications.com

SJODIN COMMUNICATIONS
A PUBLIC SPEAKING, SALES TRAINING AND CONSULTING FIRM

MONROE SEQUENCE 29